A STYLE MANUAL FOR STUDENTS

A STYLE MANUAL
FOR STUDENTS

———

EDWARD D. SEEBER

for the preparation of
term papers, essays, and theses

SECOND EDITION, *revised*

Indiana University Press
Bloomington & London

TO THE STUDENT

This guide for authors of term papers, essays, and theses explains, and illustrates with copious examples and specimen pages, present-day styling and typescript preparation, the handling of prose and verse citations, foreign-language problems (titles, proper names, word division, etc.), footnoting and bibliographical procedures, and other matters indispensable for the achievement of correctness, clarity, ease of reading, consistency, and good appearance.

It also corresponds in the main with the *MLA Style Sheet*, which has been influential in simplifying and regularizing the scholarly style of many American journals and university presses. At the same time, its sphere of usefulness extends by design beyond the humanities, even though it does not deal expressly with certain usages, especially as regards footnote citation, peculiar to some other fields. It is not dogmatic, but makes appropriate allowances for personal choice between correct alternatives, and for usages that may be prescribed or favored by a particular department or school.

Taking a realistic view of students' needs, this manual avoids unwarranted and confusing distinctions between the styling of papers or theses and the preparation of manuscripts for publication. It thus provides a useful guide to principles that can be applied, with minor adjustments, to the styling of printers' copy. A similar volume by the same author, *A Style Manual for Authors*, Midland Book No. 76 (Bloomington: Indiana University Press, 1967), contains additional information of use to writers of books or of articles for scholarly journals.

Bloomington, Indiana
March, 1964

PREFACE TO THE REVISED EDITION

Improvements in the present edition consist mainly in scattered clarifications and refinements in the text and index, some expansion in the sections on quoted matter, and a more comprehensive treatment of the effectual handling of cross references and of authors' names, pseudonyms, and titles—both English and foreign—cited in text, footnotes, bibliography, and index.

A continuing effort has been made to forgo excessive details, to introduce abundant illustrations, and to encourage, on the part of the user, a certain degree of self-reliance and discrimination.

Bloomington, Indiana
December, 1966

CONTENTS

A STYLE MANUAL FOR STUDENTS

I

GENERAL SUGGESTIONS

1 **Identical copy.** Retain an extra and *identical* copy of your typescript, containing all corrections, inserts, and other alterations.

2 **Copyreading.** Copyread your manuscript carefully (whether you do your own typing or not), checking for accuracy and consistency in usage and style, word division, punctuation, spacing, etc. Complete and verify all quotations as regards source, spelling, punctuation, accent marks, etc.

3 **Revision.** Allow some time to elapse, if possible, between your first and final drafts. Before submission, try to eliminate pompous and pedantic diction, clichés, digressions and irrelevancies, ambiguities and omissions in footnotes, unsuitable abbreviations in the text proper,* colloquialisms, meaningless words, circumlocutions, and repetitious words, phrases, or subject matter. Reduce so far as possible the number of your footnotes and lengthy quotations. Consult your dictionary frequently.

4 **Consistency.** To avoid delays, vexations, and added expense, have it clearly understood that your typist will adhere strictly to the system of styling that you have prescribed.

To achieve consistency, keep before you a list of your spellings of variable proper nouns and words like *role—rôle, co-ordinate—coördinate—coordinate, theater—theatre, wilful—*

---

* Among those to be avoided in the text are abbreviations of months (Feb.), MS for manuscript, except in references (do not say "this MS," but "MS. 16" is permissible), U.S., St. (Street), Jas. (James), Rev. ("the Rev. Jones"), Vol., p., 1st. Allowed are: Mr., Dr., St. (Saint), A.D., A.M., i.e., e.g., etc., viz., and, in parenthetical references, Vol., p., vv., cf., and the like.

willful, sizable—sizeable, per cent—percent; also forms like Mar.—March; April 1940—April, 1940; & Co. —and Co.; p. 24 n.—p. 24n.; Chap.—chap.—ch., etc. Note the use of required or optional capitals with words relating to religious denominations or sects, philosophical, literary, or artistic schools: Baptist, Epicurean, epicurean, Romantic Movement, romanticism, Naturalism, naturalist, Pre-Raphaelites, etc.

5 Corrections and insertions. If it is permissible in informal papers and reports to make last-minute corrections and insertions, these may be written (typed, if you do not write legibly) *above* the line (not in margins) or pasted (not pinned or clipped) to the page. Do not use proofreaders' marks. Indicate precisely where insertions are to be made, using a caret (∧) below the line rather than a virgule (/)—also called a "slash" or "slant"—and revise spacing, paragraphing, footnotes, etc., as required. Pages or footnotes added later are numbered 6a, 6b, etc. If you remove an entire page, say page 11, double number the preceding page (10-11) to preserve continuity of pagination. In theses and other manuscripts of permanent record, such alterations should obviously be avoided.

6 First person. It is now generally agreed that writers need have no compunction about writing in the first person. The use of "I" is honest and straightforward, does not in itself reflect vanity, and is superior to self-conscious and clumsy efforts to suggest detachment—"we do not believe," "the present writer," "this editor," etc.

7 Dictionaries. Whether you use Funk and Wagnalls' *Standard College Dictionary, The Random House Dictionary,* Webster's *New World Dictionary of the American Language, New Collegiate,* or *New International,* refer consistently to the same volume.

II

FORM OF THE MANUSCRIPT

8 Paper. Use white, fairly opaque, nonglossy paper of standard size (8½ x 11 inches). Submit no copy, even a rough draft, on onionskin paper. Readers may object to "erasable" paper because it is lacking in opacity, slippery to handle, and difficult to write on with a pen; also, it smudges easily, and Xerox copies are wanting in contrast.

For term papers and reports, a good bond paper of adequate body is satisfactory. A thesis will require, in addition to one original, several copies made by whatever process—carbon, Multilith, Xerox, etc.—is allowed by your school or department. The appearance of carbon copies will be determined by the paper selected, the kind of typewriter used, the typist's touch, and the quality and condition of the carbon paper. A satisfactory weight of paper (if a particular one is not specified by your school) is best determined by experiment. Twenty-pound stock, often recommended, may produce smudging in the third carbon copy. Sixteen-pound paper has its advocates, as does thirteen-pound—that most likely to produce clear copies. One may consider using sixteen-pound paper for the first two copies, and thirteen-pound for the rest. Rag content should be at least 50 per cent as a safeguard against eventual color changes and brittleness. The best paper has 100 per cent rag content.

9 Carbon paper. Use only a superior grade of black carbon paper. For uniformity in appearance, discard it after typing approximately five to eight pages. Uniformity can be controlled also by purchasing at one time all the paper, both white and carbon, that will be needed.

10 Type. The common type sizes are pica (10 characters to the inch) and elite (12 to the inch). Pica is sometimes specified for theses. For appearance' sake, avoid mixed type sizes and styles.

11 Margins. Leave approximately 1½ inches at top and left, and 1 inch at bottom and right. Insert paper with left edge at zero, and set margin stops at 15 and 75 for pica type, or at 18 and 90 for elite. Center of typed page will be at 45 and 54 respectively. (These directions do not apply to some electric models and foreign machines.)

12 Spacing and indention. Double space the text proper. Single space verse and long prose citations, footnotes, parts of table of contents and bibliography, and index, as explained below. Begin first line on ordinary page nine lines from top. Paragraphs are often indented seven spaces, sometimes five. For other indentions see index.

13 Page numbers are set one inch from top of page (i.e., on the sixth line) and flush with the right margin. Numbers (optional) on pages bearing section headings (Preface; Chapter I, etc.) are centered at bottom margin. Write page number without period, hyphens, or parentheses.

Consider (but do not number) the title page as page i, and use lower-case Roman for all pages preceding the first page of text. (The copyright page and table of contents are not numbered.) After page 1 (Arabic), number consecutively to last page of manuscript. Do not number the *vita* if placed at the end. On numbering of inserted pages, see section 5.

14 Blank pages and half titles. Omit blank pages except for one or two at beginning and end. Use half titles only in works divided into parts. They should precede each numbered part and each section of reference matter (appendix, bibliography, index, etc.). Write title, in capitals, slightly above center of page. Assign a page number, but omit it on the page itself.

15 Covers that are inexpensive and easily removed are suitable for term papers and the like. Papers having reference matter at the end should not be stapled. A thesis is best kept in one or more spring binders.

III

THE PARTS AND THEIR FORMS

16 Parts of the manuscript. Sections of a manuscript, each of which starts a new page, are commonly arranged in the following order: *

blank leaves
title page
copyright page
preface (or foreword)
list of abbreviations
acknowledgments
table of contents
list of illustrations
list of tables
introduction

text
appendix
notes (if typed at end)
glossary
bibliography
author index
subject index
vita (if placed at end)
blank leaves

17 Title page. Schools and departments usually prescribe the contents and layout of thesis title pages. The following directions, illustrated in specimen pages 1 and 2, represent only one of several possible forms. Center all lines on page (using 45 or 54 as center guide). Type title, if one line in length, on the tenth line from top of page. If more than one line, begin on the ninth line. Use capitals only. Underline any words that would appear in italics if printed, and omit period at end. In a long title, double space between lines and use inverted pyramid form, dividing lines, if possible, by thought groups.

* This is the usual format for books. For a thesis, check local requirements as regards order of contents, additional parts such as approval sheet, abstract, etc.

Type author's name, in capitals, twenty spaces below a single-line title, or twenty-one spaces below the first line of a multiple-line title. Two spaces above name, type BY or EDITED BY, centered, in capitals.

Matter at the bottom of the title page should preserve the usual one-inch margin. (See specimen pages.)

Title pages for short papers, reports, or essays may look pretentious unless they offer additional useful information such as name of course, section number, date, etc.

18 Preface (or foreword) (omit in table of contents). Brief remarks addressed to the reader concerning the purpose, limits, background, etc., of the study, editions, materials, or techniques employed, a *short* list of abbreviations used in the footnotes, and acknowledgments (if any)* should be put in a preface or foreword rather than in an introduction (see section 21, "Introduction"). Type heading, in capitals, at least twelve lines from top of page, and begin text from three to five lines below. A short preface should be dropped farther to give better centering on page.

19 Table of contents (see specimen pages 3-8). All copy, including the heading, should be centered vertically on page; but the heading should not be less than ten spaces from top of page, nor should the last line be less than one inch from the bottom. Three spaces below the heading, and flush with the left margin, type the word "Chapter" (initial capital only), and across the page, ending at the right margin, the word "Page." Triple space before the first entry and between all major entries (chapters, appendices, etc.). Single space

---

* Acknowledgment of special help and favors (e.g., consultation on technical matters, the loan of a manuscript, or the granting of access to private papers) is a courtesy that cannot be overlooked; but a student may without compunction refrain from expressing thanks, however heartfelt, to his thesis director or committee for their routine work. Acknowledgments should be phrased concisely and circumspectly.

An alternate device is to insert a separate, unnumbered sheet, bearing the appropriate heading, immediately before the table of contents. If a short paragraph suffices, type it on the upper portion of this insertion, and omit the heading.

in chapter headings of more than one line in length, indenting the second line two spaces.

Align chapter numbers (Roman capitals) so that the longest begins at left margin. Each is followed by a period (aligned vertically) and two spaces. Unnumbered headings (Appendix, Sources Consulted, Index, etc.) begin at left margin. Leaders (double-spaced periods) should connect the last word of chapter and main headings with page number. The first period should not appear in the first space following the heading, and the last period should not appear beyond the space preceding P in the word "Page." Align leaders vertically.

Apportion entries filling two pages of a table of contents fairly evenly. Do not repeat headings on second page, but repeat "Chapter" and "Page" ten spaces from the top. Make the first entry on this page a new chapter or major section heading, rather than a carry-over line from the first page. (See specimen pages 6, 7.)

In an analytical table of contents (which should avoid extreme complexity), separate subheadings from main headings and from each other by double spacing. Indent three spaces from first word of main heading. Indent carry-over lines two spaces, and single space. Triple space before the next main heading. Type subheadings in lower case, capitalizing important words. If numbered, use system prescribed under section 49, "Outline Form." Page references may be put in parentheses, reserving page column for main entries. (See specimen pages 3, 6-8.)

20 **Lists of illustrations and tables** follow the general form of the table of contents. Write entries, double-spaced, in capitals and lower case; single space carry-over lines and indent two spaces. Number plates in Roman capitals, figures and tables in Arabic. For best form, consult published works in your field.

21 **Introduction.** An introduction, properly considered, is a part of the text and not a substitute for the preface (q.v.). In some studies, such as critical editions, introductions are justified (see specimen pages 4, 5); but in many theses they can be dispensed with in favor of a more direct beginning in Chapter I. If preliminary matter is so treated, a suitable heading can be devised such as "The Historical Setting"; "A Half-Century of Research"; "The Ideological Background"; "Aims and Methods," etc. A historical or review-of-previous-studies approach must, of course, be confined within sensible limits. If "Introduction" is used along with numbered headings, number it also and treat it as Chapter I.

22 Chapter headings (see specimen page 9). Nine spaces from top of page, type CHAPTER I, centered, in capitals. Two spaces below write chapter title, in capitals, also centered. Omit period. If longer than one line, single space and use inverted pyramid form. Begin text three spaces below.

23 Subheadings within chapters (use these only if clearly warranted, not as mere padding) consist, in descending order of importance, of centered major headings, sideheads flush with left margin, and paragraph headings. In major headings, capitalize principal words and omit period at end. Underlining is not necessary; but if a subordinate rank of major headings is used, the more important ones may be underlined for contrast. These are usually not numbered. If a long heading would extend to the left of regular paragraph indentions, use inverted pyramid form and single space between lines. Allow three spaces above the heading and three below. Major headings may be included in table of contents.

24 Sideheads. Capitalize only the first word and proper nouns or adjectives, and omit period at end. If sidehead would extend beyond center of page, use two or more lines of approximately equal length, single spaced, and all flush with left margin. If these headings are clearly used for enumeration, they may be numbered in Arabic, followed by a period. Allow three spaces above sidehead, and two below.

Main headings and sideheads (but not paragraph headings) at the foot of a page should be followed by at least two lines of type. If this is impossible, leave the page short and resume on the next page.

In papers, centered Roman numerals (capitals) may

be used in place of chapters to indicate broad divisions. Descriptive headings are usually omitted. Divisions indicating clear breaks in context may be shown also by extra spacing, i.e., by dropping three spaces instead of the usual two.

25 Paragraph headings (underlined, but usually not numbered) start at normal paragraph indention and are run into the paragraph. Capitalize as in other sideheads, and terminate with a period or a period and dash (typed as two hyphens: - -).

26 Mottoes at heads of chapters, dropped three spaces below heading, begin slightly to the left of center of page (unless very short) and end at right margin. Omit quotation marks. Type source below text, ending at least one inch short of the right margin. Introduce source with a dash (- -) and omit period at end. Begin text three lines below.

27 Appendix. Heading and title (which should always be given) are spaced like chapter headings (q.v.); but an appendix that fills less than a page should be centered vertically. Label multiple appendices APPENDIX A, etc., in capitals, and begin each on a new page.

28 Bibliography. See chapters XII, XIII.

29 Index. Although usually not required, a good index adds greatly to the usefulness of theses that contain complex subject matter or numerous references to proper names or place names. All entries may usually be put in a single index if it is of moderate length. If not, an author index may precede the subject index. Both are listed in the table of contents. Do not index front matter preceding introduction or text.

Heading is typed nine spaces from top of page, centered. Three spaces below, single-spaced and running from left to right margins, a note may be added explaining the limitations of the index, basis of selection of items, etc. Drop three spaces for first entry.

It is easier to type indexes in a single column, but double column is permissible. In either case, single space within each entry, double space between entries. Indent carry-over lines two or three spaces, and leave three spaces between letters of the alphabet. If you use double columns, the first column should start at the left margin and the second column should end at the right margin. Lines in the two columns should be of the same maximum length, and short enough to leave a well-defined clear space vertically. Start the right-hand column two or three spaces to the right of center.

Entries may begin either with capitals (except in the case of glosses, word studies, and other special forms) or, except for proper nouns, with lower case. Use commas after entry and between page references. Omit period after last page reference. Use corrected, modernized spellings when possible, avoiding the use of "sic." The form "Chap. IV *passim*" may be used if appropriate, but specific page references are preferred. "Passim" and other words that are not index entries are underlined (for italics). Write cross references as follows: Esquemeling, Alexandre, *see* Oexmelin; but write "see also *Hamlet*" without underlining. Write titles thus: *Scots Poem, A*; *Progress of Romance, The*. Footnotes may be indicated in various ways: 56n, 76 n., 76 n. 3; 56*n*, 76 and *n*.; 39 (n. 16), 158 (nn. 38, 39).

Consult, on this subject, Sina Spiker, *Indexing Your Book. A Practical Guide for Authors* (Madison: University of Wisconsin Press, 1964), and the Chicago *Manual of Style*, section "Indexes." As a general guide to form, see the index to the present volume. On names of persons and the use of cross references, see below, sections 112-13, 115-17.

30 Vita, in theses, should contain the following minimal information: full name, place and date of birth, educational background and degrees (with a list of professors under whom the candidate studied for advanced degrees), and previous occupations and employment. The *vita* is not numbered, and is not included in the table of contents.

IV

PUNCTUATION AND THE MECHANICS OF WRITING

31 Comma. Use a comma (*a*) before and after the abbreviations "i.e.," "e.g.," and "viz.," but not preceding "such as"; (*b*) to separate independent clauses (unless they are extremely short or have the same subject) joined by a pure conjunction (*and, but, or, for, neither, nor, yet, so*), noting that this rule concerns *clauses* so joined, not verbs (cf. "He finished the play in March and published it in April"); (*c*) to separate subordinate clauses that either precede or follow the main clause, unless they are short and closely related in thought;* (*d*) in nonrestrictive clauses (those that can be omitted without changing the meaning of the main clause), e.g., "His first novel, which cost him his health, was never published" (cf. "The novel which cost him his health was his best").

In series containing three or more parts, final commas before "and" or "or" are recommended for clarity (e.g., "red, black, and blue pennants"; "the *History* was printed for Ball, Taylor, and Osborn"), notwithstanding a growing tendency to dispense with them. A comma may usually be omitted in an appositive used to distinguish its principal from other persons or things called by the same name, e.g., "the poet Young," "in his novel *Ivanhoe*"; but cf. "in her next novel, *Virginia.*"

---

* For further elucidation of this and other points of grammar and correct usage, the student should own a modern work like Porter G. Perrin, K. W. Dykema, and W. R. Ebbitt, *Writer's Guide and Index to English*, 4th ed. (Chicago: Scott, Foresman & Co., 1965). Consult also the Chicago *Manual of Style*, section "Punctuation," and the index.

32 Spacing. Leave *one* space after commas, colons, and semi-colons. Leave *two* spaces after periods and other terminal punctuation, e.g., between sentences and after periods following number or letter before a main section heading. *Exceptions*: one space is more pleasing after certain forms like "p. 45, n. 6." Do not space after the first period in most abbreviations: A.D., A.M. (a.m.), N.Y., U.S., Ph.D., P.S., e.g., i.e., n.p., n.d.; but space after initials of persons (R. A. Jones) unless initials alone are used (R.A.J.).

33 Hyphen. Hyphens are used mainly

- in compound numbers from twenty-one to ninety-nine
- between compound adjectival modifiers preceding nouns (e.g., a well-known man; an up-to-date process; single-spaced lines; second- and third-year courses), but not with proper nouns (e.g., a New England winter), unambiguous adverbs, especially those ending in *-ly* (e.g., an ever changing .scene; a hastily written essay), or modifiers that follow nouns (e.g., a man well known for his charity; a process that is up to date)
- to separate identical vowels resulting from prefixion (e.g., re-educate, supra-auditory, semi-invalid, co-ordinal; but note the present trend to write "cooperate" and "coordinate"). A dieresis over *e* or *o* may replace the hyphen (e.g., preëminent)
- to distinguish meaning (e.g., recreation, re-creation; reformation, re-formation; recount, re-count, etc.)
- in a limited number of miscellaneous compounds (e.g., D-Day, self-sufficiency, half-wit, loud-speaker, make-up, pitter-patter, un-co-operative, non-coöperation).

Bear in mind (*a*) that hyphens are optional in some words (e.g., weekend, nearby, today, goodbye); (*b*) that the trend in present-day American usage (though this is not apparent in the more traditional manuals and dictionaries) is toward fewer hyphenated words (cf. office seeker, hero worship, fellow man, cross reference, songbird, antisocial, coauthor, extralegal, nonfictional, postclassical); (*c*) that a dictionary is indispensable for guidance in the correct use of hyphens and of separate and solid words (e.g., news room, newsstand, master stroke, masterwork, water level, watermark, etc.).

34 Dash. Distinguish between a hyphen (-) and a dash (—), indicated in typing by two hyphens (- -), noting the use of the latter with dates in the sense of "to" (see section 38, line 2), and—as used here—with parenthetical remarks. Neither is preceded nor followed by a space, and a comma and dash are not used together. A four-hyphen dash (- - - -) is used where a sentence is left unfinished or ends abruptly (e.g., in dialogue), and for an omitted word or part of a word; but in proper nouns written with omitted letters, hyphens may be used to represent these letters, if known, e.g., L - - d K - - - s (Lord Kames), H - - - shire (Hampshire). If the exact word is unknown, use a prolonged dash. In titles and quoted matter, follow the original form, e.g., *Histoire de Mademoiselle de* ❋ ❋ ❋.

35 Quotation marks. Double quotation marks are preferred for general use, and single quotation marks for quotations within quotations, linguistic citations, and other limited usages. Punctuate as follows: commas and periods *precede* quotation marks, including the combination (' ") at the end of a quotation within a quotation. But with single words and phrases, and in bibliographical description, the preferred placement of the *single* quotation mark is: *deshielo* 'thaw', "A Misreading of Poe's 'Ligeia'," "*Jalousie* appears to be a . . . form of the traditional 'psychological novel'."

Semicolons and colons *follow* quotation marks. Use care in placing question or exclamation marks in relation to quotation marks according to the sense required (e.g., He asked, "Are you coming?" Is it true that "Absence makes the heart grow fonder"?). Foreign quotation marks (e.g., French or German), which are both shaped and punctuated differently from ours, are not used with passages cited in an English text.

36 Parentheses. In parenthetical matter beginning with a capital (i.e., following terminal punctuation), the period should precede the last parenthesis. *Example*: (First edition, 1831.)

In other cases, period follows. *Example*: . . . in 1840 (first published in 1831). See also section 66.

37 Square brackets, rather than parentheses, should enclose

- words, letters, dates, etc., interpolated by the writer within quoted matter, e.g., ". . . was a frequent visitor in his [Swift's] home"; ". . . had give[n]"; also interpolations in bibliographical matter, e.g., descriptive titles and clarifications in titles (see section 120, first entries in paragraphs 8-10), appended remarks such as "[Rev. art.]," etc.

- dates, page numbers, and other data relating to published material, lacking or incorrect in the original and supplied by the writer, e.g., [Paris], 1710; [c. 1630]; p. 149 [for 194]; [David Henshaw], *The Triumphs of Europe*

- parenthetical matter falling within parentheses. This is sometimes unavoidable, but in the commonest occurrences —e.g., (*New Verse*, XI [Oct. 1934], 8); (*The Eccentric Design* [New York, 1959], p. 10)—commas are often substituted (see section 106, sample note 28)

- phonetic transcription

- the word "sic."*

If typewriter is not equipped with brackets, they can be added neatly by hand. Although the improvised form made with virgule and underscores (   ) is widely favored, it is likely to result in poor spacing, especially when enclosing a single letter or digit.

38 Dates and numerals. Note the following forms: April-May, 1940; April 5, 1940 - - June 5, 1941; from January 1 to March 15; the 6th of July. Be consistent in using alternate forms: June 5, 1941 or 5 June 1941; June 1941 or June, 1941. If a comma precedes the year date, another follows if the sentence continues: "On June 1, 1855, he. . . ." Write "382 B.C.," but "A.D. 405," to agree with the reading "*anno Domini* 405."

---

* "Sic" may properly be used to call attention to errors, misspellings, etc.—especially if these might be mistaken for typists' errors; but avoid overuse with mere archaisms and frequent misspellings in certain classes of quoted matter.

Spell out (*a*) a number or date that begins a sentence, (*b*) numbers of less than three digits except dates, page numbers, connected groups (of numbers, dimensions, distances, sums of money, etc.), and numbers used in footnotes, (*c*) round numbers (e.g., three hundred, fifteen hundred, four thousand).

Use commas in numbers having four or more digits, except in dates and page numbers. Write "the 1840's" (or "1840s"), "the forties" (but not "the 40's"), "sixteenth-century poetry" (not "16th").

Inclusive page numbers and dates may be written in full or in condensed form, e.g., 162-70, 1830-35. (The *MLA Style Sheet* allows this for dates but would have page numbers through 999 written in full.) When the first number ends in two ciphers, write the second number in full (e.g., 1600-1648); when the last digit but one in the first number is a cipher, write either the final digit of the second number (e.g., 102-3, 1604-5) or the entire second number (102-103, 1604-1605). Do not write "1604-05."

39 Possessives. Formation of the possessive case in words ending in a sibilant (*s, z*) is not uniform, but the following procedures may be used for consistency: in one-syllable words, add *'s* (Keats's, Voss's, James's); in words of two or more syllables, add apostrophe but omit *s* (Dickens', Simonides', duchess', for conscience' sake), also in plural forms that add *-es* to a singular form ending in *s, sh, ch, x,* or *z* (Churches', Joneses', Knoxes'). In foreign names, follow the same rule after determining whether or not the final *s* is pronounced (Solis', Mme de Genlis', Dumas's, Ninon de Lenclos's).

Avoid the possessive with titles ("*The Mill on the Floss's* conclusion") and, generally, with inanimate objects ("the academy's members," "the Tower of London's interior"), noting common exceptions ("a day's journey," "for appearance' sake," etc.).

40 Word division at ends of typed lines (to be avoided whenever possible) is governed by strict rules of syllabication and, at the same time, by conventions bearing upon good appearance. The right-hand margin is flexible, therefore try to avoid (*a*) more than two consecutive lines ending in hyphens, (*b*) separation of single letters (*a-bridge, man-y, é-té, a-stro*), (*c*) carry-over of two letters (*hearti-ly, delight-ed, au-be, chari-té, Zwischenpau-se*), (*d*) further division of words already hyphenated (*daugh-ter-in-law, au-des-sus, Saint-Laurent, lobens-würd-dig*), (*e*) divisions of names of persons, a first and last name, and initials and last name, (*f*) word fragments at the end of a paragraph or page. Do not divide words of one syllable or integral combinations like A.D. 825, numbers (Arabic or Roman), etc.

41 English words are divided as follows:

1. In the United States (but not in Great Britain) the division is primarily on the basis of sound: the pronunciation of the line-end fragment must be compatible with that of the whole word. Thus syllabication will often be at variance with etymology: *finan-cier, bibliog-raphy, philol-ogy, perso-nae, ambig-uous, prec-ipice, chil-dren.*

2. They may, however, divide in accordance with etymology, meaning, and sound: *biblio-phile, philo-logical, person-ify, ambi-guity, pre-fix, child-ish.*

3. Words sometimes divide immediately before a suffix (*wish-ing, judg-ment, blu-ish, hum-ble, social-ism*), sometimes not (*tack-ling, stop-ping, tick-lish, witti-cism, sati-rist*).

4. Double like consonants usually divide (*Rus-sian, dif-ficult*), but not always (*dress-ing, dull-ard, all-over, pass-ably*).

For further refinements, see the Chicago *Manual of Style.* When in doubt about syllabication, consult any of the latest dictionaries.

42 French words are divided as follows:

1. A single consonant between vowels (including the nasalized vowels *an, en, in, on, un,* etc.) goes with the following syllable: *co-mé-die, a-mou-reux, cir-con-ven-tion, main-te-nant.*

2. Two consecutive consonants usually divide: *bap-tême, empor-tent, tor-til-lage;* but two unlike consonants, the second of which is *l* or *r*, belong with the following syllable:

éta-blir, pro-créer, ven-tre-bleu. Exceptions are *n* in a nasalized vowel (*ban-lieue, ron-ron*), and *rl, lr*, which always divide (*par-ler, mer-luche, Mal-raux*).

3. In words containing three consecutive consonants, the first two usually end a syllable, and the other goes with the next syllable: *Alc-mène, comp-tais, ponc-tué, ving-tième*. Exceptions are the combinations consonant-plus-*l* or *r*, which ordinarily begin a syllable: *ar-brisseau, es-clan-dre*. Words containing a prefix may follow the general rule: *ins-truit, cons-tant, subs-tance, trans-pirer*; but it is equally correct to divide between prefix and root: *in-struit, con-stant, sub-stance, tran-spirer*.

4. Two consonants representing one sound do not divide: *tou-cher, or-phi-que, mono-thé-isme*.

5. The commonplace liquid sound *gn* is never divided (*ma-gni-fique, monta-gne*); but in certain less commonly used words of learned or foreign origin these consonants, pronounced separately, are divided: *diag-nostique, stag-nation, reg-nicole*, etc.

43 Italian words are divided as follows:

1. A single consonant between vowels goes with the following syllable: *do-ma-ni, li-be-ra-to-re*.

2. Double like consonants are divided: *repub-blica, at-tiz-zamento*.

3. Two consonants, the first of which is *l, m, n,* or *r*, are divided: *al-bero, lam-pada, man-dare, por-porato*.

4. Other combinations of two consonants go with the following syllable: *da-gli, antipa-sto, monta-gne, chiaro-scuro*; but consonants that cannot be pronounced together are divided: *prag-matismo, op-tare, seg-mento, dog-matico*.

5. The first of three consonants, except *s*, goes with the preceding syllable: *com-prare, Lon-dra, sem-preverde, chiac-chierare*; but *di-stributivo, e-straneo*.

6. Diphthongs containing an unstressed *i* or *u* are never divided: *giu-sto, gio-varsi, uo-mini, Eu-ropa, princi-pio*. (Certain vowel combinations can divide because they are not true diphthongs: *pa-esano, co-eterno*.)

44 Spanish words are divided as follows:

1. A word has as many syllables as it has vowels or diph-thongs: *ba-úl, an-ti-ci-par-se, o-pe-ra-cio-nes, ca-lien-te.*

2. A single consonant between vowels goes with the fol-lowing syllable: *i-ma-gi-na-ble, a-le-mán, espa-ñol.*

3. *ch, ll,* and *rr* go with the following syllable: *le-che, ta-llador, papa-rrucha.*

4. Two consonants between vowels usually divide: *ac-ción, in-negable, nin-guno, os-ten-toso, or-nato.*

5. *l* and *r* go with a preceding consonant: *a-blan-dar, re-trac-tación, fil-tración;* but prepositional prefixes form sep-arate syllables: *sub-lunar, des-re-glado.*

6. In the combination *s* plus a consonant, the *s* goes with the preceding syllable, prefix or not: *es-labón, abs-tener.*

45 German words are divided as follows:

1. A single consonant and groups of consonants which represent single sounds (*ch, sch, ph, th, st*) go with the fol-lowing syllable: *Li-te-ra-tur, Mär-chen, Spre-cher, For-schung, Stro-phen, ka-tholisch, Mei-ster.*

2. Other consonant groups are usually divided: *Hun-ger, ir-gend, im-mer, interes-sieren.*

3. If *ck* is divided, spelling changes to *k-k: stückeln—stük-keln. Tz* is divided *t-z: blit-zen.*

4. Compound words are divided into their component parts: *Ver-ein, Manu-script, Falsch-heit, blut-rot, ehr-bar.*

5. In foreign words, *b, d, g, k, p, t* plus *l* or *r* are carried over: *Pu-blikum, Me-trum, Ma-krone.*

46 Russian words. Russian and other Slavic words (including transliterations) divide in an involved manner that can best be explained by a person conversant with them.

47 Latin words are divided as follows:

1. A consonant between vowels goes with the following syllable (*pe-cu-nia, fi-gu-ra*) except when there is a prefix present: *ab-orior, prod-eo, per-inde.*

2. Double consonants usually divide: *tris-tis, bel-lum;* but *b, p, d, t, g, c, ch, ph, th* plus *l* or *r* are carried over: *pa-tribus, ne-glectum, mi-thrax, a-phron.*

3. When there are more than two consonants between vowels, all but the first go with the following syllable (*mon-strum, claus-tra*) except when there is a prefix present: *trans-gressus, post-habeo.* Words containing the combination *l, m, n, r* plus *ct, ps, pt* are sometimes divided between the second and third letters: *consump-tus, farc-tus.*

4. Two contiguous vowels or a vowel and a diphthong can be divided: *the-atrum, de-aeque.*

48 **Greek words** divide according to the same general principles as do Latin words.

49 **Outline form** (this does not apply to chapter subheadings) commonly follows this style: *

I. Expository aphorisms
II. Paradoxical aphorisms
   A. Polar paradoxical aphorisms
      1. Polar aphorisms of parallel structure
         a. parallelism of antithesis
         b. parallelism of analysis
         c. parallelism of synthesis
      2. Polar aphorisms of equational structure
      3. Polar aphorisms of comparative structure
   B. Non-Polar paradoxical aphorisms

Further divisions under *c*, above, would be introduced, in order, by (1), (a), (i), etc. Note that a minimum of two is logically required for each rank, i.e., I implies a II, 1 implies a 2, etc. A single heading is otherwise absorbed into the heading immediately preceding it.

* The illustration is from an article by Harold E. Pagliaro in *PMLA,* LXXIX (1964), 45 n.

V

TITLES CITED IN TEXT AND IN FOOTNOTES

50 Form of title. Take book title from title page only. Take title of article from title page of article itself, not from table of contents. Add punctuation (often omitted in printed titles) as needed to avoid ambiguity or confusion, e.g., *Sidney's Appearance: A Study in Elizabethan Portraiture*. Give a title in its original form, even though it seems wrong or at variance with common practice: retain original spellings and archaisms like *Compleat, De Foe,* French *Avantures,* using "sic" only after misspellings and other errors that might appear to be your own (see section 111, paragraph 7, second entry). Special circumstances may require the use of translated or transliterated titles (see section 120, paragraph 12, third entry).

Underline (to indicate italics) titles and subtitles of books (but not the Bible or books thereof), pamphlets, plays, separately published poems (regardless of length),* and periodicals. In mentioning a periodical or newspaper, one need not treat a definite article or the name of a city as part of the title (e.g., "in the *Indiana Quarterly for Bookmen*"; "in the Chicago *Tribune*"); but bibliographical citations should read *The Chicago Tribune,* etc. Enclose a title within a title in quotation marks, e.g., *Textual Studies of Goethe's "Faust."* Do not underline punctuation marks (except apostrophes) or spaces between words (except in hyphenated words when both parts are in the same line).

---

* If the history of publication cannot be readily ascertained, one may italicize titles of long poems, and enclose those of short poems in quotation marks.

51 Poems, articles, theses, etc. Titles of poems not published separately, articles, chapters, sections or essays in a volume by several authors, and unpublished theses are enclosed in quotation marks and not underlined. Book titles that figure in such titles are underlined for italics, e.g., "Plutarch and Rousseau's First *Discours*."

52 Names of series or particular editions are not underlined and need not be in quotation marks or parentheses. (See section 89, and section 106, sample notes 9, 10.)

53 English titles. Capitalize all words except prepositions, conjunctions, and articles, unless one of these is the first or the last word (the longer prepositions, like "toward," are sometimes capitalized). Capitalize any word following a colon. Usage varies as regards hyphenated compounds, and not all writers observe the Chicago *Manual of Style* rule that only nouns and proper adjectives, in the second component, are capitalized (e.g., *High-Speed Trains*; but *Fifty-first Street, English-speaking Peoples*, etc.). Hyphenated words that are considered to be one word rather than a compound are often capitalized as follows: *"If"-clauses, Dumb-show, the A-text, Gold-mine, Well-being, Self-scrutiny*, etc.

54 French and Italian titles allow great latitude as regards capitalization. Follow these acceptable rules for consistency. Capitalize an initial article, the noun following, and an adjective that may come between, e.g., *Les Femmes savantes; Le Grand Dictionnaire géographique; Piccolo Mondo antico.* A proper noun or a noun used metaphorically may be capitalized, e.g., "Documents inédits sur l'Hôtel de Bourgogne"; *Le Rouge et le Noir; La République des Lettres.* If a title begins with a word other than an article or an adjective, subsequent words (with the exception of proper nouns) are not capitalized, e.g., *De l'amitié; Sur la pierre blanche; Sull'oceano; Alle porte d'Italia.* See other examples below, sections 106, 120. The same form has long been favored in France and Italy for periodical titles (*La Nouvelle Revue française; Revue de littérature comparée; Giornale italiano di filologia*); but a number of editors here and abroad now use additional capitals (*Revue des Lettres Modernes; Giornale Storico della Letteratura Italiana*). Use one form consistently.

55 Spanish titles. Capitalize the first word only in a book title (*La verdad sospechosa; Amor con vista*). Periodical titles, here and abroad, often use additional capitals (*La España Moderna; Nueva Revista de Filología*); but forms like *Revista española de teología* are not uncommon. Use one form consistently.

56 German titles. Capitalize all nouns, e.g., *Zwölf mittelhochdeutsche Minnelieder und Reimreden.* See other examples below, section 120, paragraphs 2, 3, 4, 7.

57 Greek and Latin titles. Capitalize the first word only, also proper nouns and adjectives based thereon, e.g., *Archivum Romanicum.* Additional capitals may be used in postclassical works, e.g., *Eikon Basilike; Pro se Defensio* (Milton); *Biographia Literaria* (Coleridge). On punctuation, see section 96.

VI

FOREIGN WORDS AND PHRASES

58 Underlining. Isolated words and phrases originating with the author are underlined if regarded as truly foreign (e.g., *aficionado, pasticcio, quatrocento, chacun à son goût, pièce à thèse, Zeitgeist*). Those already naturalized (e.g., mores, a priori, leitmotif, literati, cliché, résumé) are not underlined. The list is subject to periodic revision.*

Do not underline (*a*) quotations in a foreign language, (*b*) words or phrases quoted or used in a particular sense by an author, school, etc. (e.g., Goethe's concept of *Faust* as a "rhapsodisches Drama"), (*c*) names of foreign institutions, buildings, etc., or foreign titles preceding proper names (e.g., Opernhaus; Real Museo de Pinturas; Académie de Marseille; the Champs-Elysées; le Père Charlevoix). It follows that, except for titles within titles and a few special situations, there is no need for underlining and using quotation marks around the same word.

59 Accent marks. If your typewriter does not have foreign accent marks or a dieresis, add them neatly by hand (do not use typed apostrophes or quotation marks). Omit French and Spanish (but not Italian) accents on capitals. Supply by hand umlaut on German letters (including capitals), and the character β if needed to reproduce quotations and titles exactly.

60 Ligatures in capitalized Old English and foreign words may

* Foreign words are no longer designated as such in some of the latest dictionaries, but they are plainly marked in *The Random House Dictionary, Webster's New World Dictionary,* and in the older *Collegiate* and unabridged.

be suggested thus: AElfred, OEuvres; otherwise write "waeter," "coeur," etc., without attempting to join letters in typing. Ligatures are not used in quotations from Latin, in Anglicized derivatives from Latin, or from Greek through Latin (e.g., *Aeneid*, Aeschylus, Oedipus, subpoena).

VII

QUOTED MATTER IN TEXT

61 Effective quoting. Quotations have important functions in scholarly writing, and some papers and theses require more than others; yet a proliferation of citations (and, as a result, of footnotes) does not in itself reflect thorough and meticulous scholarship, or good writing. A common product of note-taking is a stock of apt and tentatively usable quotations; but these must be introduced skilfully and as sparingly as possible.

Avoid direct quotations, both short and long, that contain nothing beyond bare factual content to warrant verbatim citation. Present the content, with appropriate indications of source, in your own words: it will be more succinct and readable, and will likely require fewer footnotes.

Avoid a string of quotations, all of which say essentially the same thing, as a device to prove or reinforce a point or argument.

Avoid raw, lengthy quotations that readers will find repellent, onerous, and, in some degree, a waste of time. Delete superfluous and irrelevant words and sentences (indicating ellipses), and paraphrase wherever possible.

A clarifying interpolation in a quoted text must not becloud or distort the original phraseology: "In his [Arnold's] home," "The exploits of my hero [Itanoko]," are preferred to "In [Arnold's] home," "The exploits of [Itanoko]."

In general, quote from foreign authors in the original, using translation and transliteration only as a practical necessity.

When you compose an English sentence that incorporates quoted matter, make sure that the whole is syntactically sound. For example, the subjunctive in "Florian doit à Rousseau le paradoxe qui veut que l'amour *soit* éternel en naissant" does not read correctly in the hybrid sentence "Florian owed to Rousseau the notion that 'l'amour *soit* éternel en naissant'." Similar incongruities can be remedied in various ways: one of the best—as the foregoing example should suggest—is to avoid any quotation that can readily be paraphrased in English.

62 Best edition. Many texts are unsuitable for ordinary quoting, e.g., unauthorized and pirated editions, cheap-paper classics and popular translations of the nineteenth century, school editions, many modern paperbacks, and obsolete editions. Select carefully the best text for your purpose, seeking advice when in doubt. If the desired text is unobtainable through interlibrary loan, microfilm copy, etc., another edition or, if need be, a translation may suffice; but do not assume that the text of one edition is identical—or even similar —to that of another. If appropriate, explain in the preface or in a footnote your use of a second-choice text.

63 Typing quotations. Run into the text, with quotation marks, all prose quotations less than four typed lines in length unless they can be typed seriatim (sometimes interspersed with longer quotations) or require special emphasis. Separate from the context quotations of four or more lines in length, drop three spaces, and single space; omit quotation marks, except those that may occur in the original. Double space between paragraphs, and triple space before resuming text.

Manuals of style often recommend that long (single-spaced) citations be indented four or five spaces from the left margin, or three spaces from both margins, allowing seven spaces (as in the main text) for paragraphing. This arrangement, which has some esthetic appeal and many devotees, is none the less troublesome, invites many short quotations, and adds only a modicum of clarity. In theses at least, given a choice, it would seem sensible to save effort and space by bringing long quotations to normal left and right margins—as many books are printed. For paragraphing, see section 69.

64 Capitalization. Although quotations must be scrupulously reproduced with respect to wording, spelling, and punctuation, it is common practice to alter capital and lower-case letters introducing them, e.g., "It is apparent that 'as they part, Hugh is angry . . .'" ("as," in the original, was capitalized); ". . . summed them up thus: 'The picture which the novelist drew . . .'" ("the," in the original, was not capitalized). Similarly the first word of a long, single-spaced quotation, introduced by a colon or following a period, may be capitalized though not so written in the original. It is correct also, in this case, to begin with the original lower-case word, preceded, at left margin, by an ellipsis sign (. . .). Follow one style consistently.

65 Italics. Unless there is a special reason (as in a critical edition) for indicating the original typography, quotations from early books in which proper names, prefaces, etc., are printed in italics may be written without underlining.

66 Parenthetical references. Parenthetical source references in short prose quotations precede a final period, e.g., ". . . of his own" (p. 6). If other terminal punctuation occurs, omit period, e.g., ". . . of his own!" (p. 6) In a long (single-spaced) prose quotation, reference follows terminal punctuation, e.g., . . . of his own. (p. 6) or [p. 6] See section 75, paragraph 2, (d).

67 Verse quotations of a single line may be run in the text with quotation marks unless they require unusual emphasis. Two lines may be so treated, separated by a virgule (/). Longer passages are dropped three spaces and centered on page, the margin being determined in general by the longest line. If lines are of unusual length, indent five spaces and indent carry-over lines an additional three to five spaces. (For further particulars, consult the Chicago *Manual of Style.*) Use single spacing and no quotation marks unless they occur in the original. Triple space after last line. (See specimen page 10.)

Line reference may, if space allows, follow the last line quoted, with no period, e.g.,

Lies buried in this lonely place. (vv. 30-32)

Reference to longer lines may be dropped two spaces, flush with the right-hand margin of the quoted matter. Titles, divisions, etc., are written similarly: (*Inferno*, X, 87) or (*Inferno* X.87), (trans. B. Q. Morgan), etc. In extended citations from poems usually printed with numbered lines, use like numbers in the right margin. References to a particular volume may be omitted if the lines quoted can be found readily in various editions; but if line numbers or other details do not agree with editions usually cited (e.g., the Globe Shakespeare), the source used should be specified.

68 Ellipses at the beginning of or within a sentence or line of verse, quoted title, etc., are indicated by three periods. Leave one space at either end of the ellipsis sign (except next to quotation marks) and *between each period*. *Example*: He says that "they ignore the modern . . . trends." (Note that no ellipsis is shown before "they," where there is an earlier omission.) As pointed out above, two other forms are possible: "He says: 'They ignore the modern . . . trends,'" and, somewhat more labored, "He says: '. . . they ignore the modern . . . trends.'" A comma, semicolon, or colon may precede or follow the ellipsis, separated from the nearest period by one space.

To indicate an ellipsis following a complete sentence, or between two sentences, use three spaced periods in addition to the sentence period. If ellipsis occurs *after* the conclusion of the first sentence, leave no space before the first of the four periods (the sentence period). A space *before* the first period denotes an omission prior to the sentence period (the fourth period). *Example*: "The confusion is immense. . . . There is no rigorous measure . . . ." Since the fourth period in the latter case represents terminal punctuation, a question or exclamation mark may be substituted as required.

In extended French and Spanish texts, indicate ellipsis by three *unspaced* periods, with one space preceding and following, e.g., "La Bruyère ... soutient la même cause. ..." In Italian texts, use four unspaced periods for all ellipses, or three following a punctuation mark. No space precedes, but one space follows, e.g., "L'italiano moderno, la lingua che si studia oggi nelle scuole,... è.... una lingua convenzionale...." Do not use these patterns with incidental foreign quotations in an English text.

Show omission of one or more lines of verse or of one or more paragraphs in a long prose citation by a row of triple-spaced periods equal in length to the longest line quoted. Indicate omissions at beginning and end of verse citations as follows:

> . . . why Man restrains
> His fiery course . . . .

69 Paragraphing. In a long quotation, indent the first word five spaces if it begins a paragraph (see specimen page 10). If it does not, start at the left margin of the quoted passage with a capital (no ellipsis sign), or with an ellipsis sign followed by a lower-case word. If, in a quotation composed of consecutive paragraphs, an ellipsis occurs at the beginning of any paragraph other than the first, begin with an ellipsis sign at the usual indention, followed by a capitalized or lower-case word as required.

One need not be overscrupulous about accounting for original paragraphing. A footnote reading "pp. 18, 25" may properly refer to a continuous passage quoted in the text and broken only by an ellipsis sign. Several passages may, within the bounds of intelligibility, be so treated.

70 Titles of persons, such as "Mr.," "Dr.," "Professor," are commonly omitted in references to prominent authors under discussion, scholars cited, or deceased persons, though they are appropriate in more personal references, acknowledgments, etc. The titles "Miss" and "Mrs." (also omitted by some) may be replaced by a given name. Retain conventional titles with certain eminent names, e.g., Mrs. Browning, Mme de Maintenon, Dr. Johnson, Sir Walter (Scott), etc.

71 End of page. Main headings and sideheads, poem titles, incomplete couplets, tercets, and quatrains should not occur in the last line of a page, and the last line of a verse or single-spaced prose citation should not be relegated to the page following.

VIII

FOOTNOTE REFERENCES IN TEXT

72 Placement. Use care in selecting the most natural and logical place for footnote reference numbers. References to quoted matter are usually put at the end of the quoted text, rather than after the author's name or an introductory phrase (see specimen page 10).

73 Numbering. In a paper, including one with numbered divisions, number the notes consecutively throughout. In a thesis, number them consecutively by chapters. Multiple notes on technical textual matters (as in a critical edition) are placed before ordinary notes, and use as references lower-case Roman a, b, c, etc., repeating after z is reached. These letters may *precede* punctuation and quotation marks. If used next to a regular footnote reference number, separate with a comma, with no spacing. In exceptional cases it is expedient to repeat the same reference number one or more times on a single page, or to use multiple references (e.g., *dervis*[a,b]), thus avoiding repetitious footnotes.

Raise footnote reference numbers in the text slightly above the line of type. Do not use parentheses. Numbers should *follow* punctuation and quotation marks. *Examples*: . . . papers.[2] . . . papers.)[2] . . . papers";[2] etc.

74 Symbols. The special footnote symbols *, †, ‡, §, ¶, #, especially useful after algebraic notations or wherever reference numbers would be confusing or inapt, are suitable also for papers or works like the present manual that have few footnotes. They may be used also for certain kinds of occasional footnotes in a work that has, at the same time, a number of ordinary footnotes using numerical references. These symbols may be doubled or tripled, thus providing eighteen references; but in practice few are usually needed, for they are used in sequence only on a single page, i.e., one note on page 2 and one note on page 3 will each be designated by a single asterisk.

IX

FOOTNOTES

75 Effective footnoting. Footnotes serve mainly to give (*a*) sources of quotations, opinions, and important facts cited in the text, and (*b*) the author's comments and explanations, additional facts, editorial and critical apparatus, technical data, etc., which, though relevant, would seem labored or distracting in the text itself. Bear in mind that footnotes result inevitably in continual (and often unrewarding) distractions to the reader, and that they should therefore be used as sparingly as is consistent with need, effectiveness, and clarity. Avoid, if possible, multiple footnotes in any one sentence.

Avoid notes (*a*) that are not strictly relevant and essential, especially sources for facts that are of common knowledge or easily verified, (*b*) that repeat unnecessarily the substance of previous notes or textual matter, (*c*) that may be combined with adjacent notes (often accomplished effectively by rewording the text, rearranging material, or grouping several consecutive references), (*d*) that can be replaced in the text by short, parenthetical references to works frequently cited,* also by remarks like "italics added,"† (*e*) that are overlong: many long notes can be eliminated or at least shortened by adding information in the text, (*f*) that are of extreme length or complexity (such matter, if indispensable, may be put into one or more appendices or in the bibliography).

* Avoid overextending this practice to references that belong properly in footnotes. Notes in the text proper must not distract the reader or suggest that two discrepant systems of footnoting are in use.

† Use italics for emphasis as little as possible in text and in quoted matter.

Use cross references sparingly; usually they should point forward rather than back.

A source reference usually precedes a quotation or remark introduced by the author's name or its equivalent; if not so introduced, it may follow. (See section 106, sample footnotes 27-34.)

76 Multiple references. If a footnote contains references to several authors or titles, separate these with semicolons, e.g., Smith, p. 10; Jones, p. 2.

77 Placement. Footnotes typed at the bottom of the page are the most convenient for readers; but in a paper it may be permissible to place them at the end, preceding the bibliography. Because most theses are now microfilmed, their footnotes are best distributed by pages.

One space below the last line of text, and beginning at the left margin, type a solid line ten to fifteen spaces in length.* Drop two spaces for the first note. Indent footnote number three to five spaces. Raise it slightly above the type line (with no space following) or, if local custom permits, put it on the type line, followed by a period and two spaces (see specimen pages 9-11).

Single space within each note and between paragraphs thereof, but double space between successive notes. Begin each note with a capital (except for glosses, definitions, and quotations beginning with an ellipsis sign) and end with terminal punctuation. Carry the second and succeeding lines to left margin.

A horizontal arrangement of two or three very short notes is permitted (see specimen page 11), but none may be carried over to the next line. On pages where there are many short notes, they may be arranged in two columns, the first number in the second column following the last number in the first column. Place the second column halfway between the beginning of the first column and the right-hand margin.

78 Overrunning page. If a note cannot be ended without overrunning the bottom margin, complete it at the foot of the

---

* This form is by no means standardized: one manual will prefer a solid line from left to right margins, another will omit the line altogether.

next page, immediately preceding notes for that page. In this case a solid line separating completed note and text can be typed from margin to margin. Such a note should be broken within a sentence to make the reader aware of the carry-over. (See specimen page 11.)

79 **Prose citations** several lines or paragraphs in length are not dropped two spaces, but are run in the text of the footnote, with quotation marks at beginning and end. Intervening paragraphs begin, but do not end, with quotation marks. Do not double space between paragraphs.

80 **Verse citations** of one or two lines may be run in the text of a footnote; otherwise, center lines on page and omit quotation marks. Leave two spaces before and after. Source may be indicated parenthetically one space below the last line, ending approximately below the last letter of the longest line quoted.

81 **First references** to published books and articles should give all pertinent bibliographical details. As an aid to the reader, repeat this form at the first recurrence of the reference in succeeding chapters. The remainder of this chapter shows the correct order of details, subject to possible omissions consistent with the form and sense of a given note.

82 **Author's name** is written with given name or initials first, and is followed by a comma. Use the name by which the author is best known, i.e., (*a*) give the fullest form used in the work cited (e.g., Paul Elmer More rather than Paul More or Paul E. More); (*b*) omit unused first and middle names (e.g., *Harry* Sinclair Lewis; *Francis* Scott *Key* Fitzgerald); (*c*) use customary modern spellings of older names (e.g., Defoe rather than De Foe); (*d*) choose the best-known name of a titled person (e.g., Benjamin Disraeli rather than Lord Beaconsfield; Lord Chesterfield rather than Philip Dormer Stanhope); (*e*) normalize an author's name preceding (but not contained within) a foreign title (e.g., in citing a French edition of the *Decameron*, write "Boccaccio" rather than "Boccace"). Omit authors' names that would appear self-evident in repeated titles; also those obviously associated with works by a particular author under discussion or with titles such as *Hamlet,* the *Divine Comedy,* or the *Aeneid.*

If you have a bibliography, let it serve to amplify single or simplified names used in your footnotes (e.g., Dante, Voltaire, Goethe, T. S. Eliot). *If you have no bibliography,* footnotes must serve in its stead by giving authors' names (the first time cited) in appropriately expanded form—for example, by replacing a first initial, if possible, by a given name as an aid to the reader. On bibliographical form, see sections 112, 115-17.

If a work has several authors, give the first name, followed by "and others" or "et al." (All the names may be given if there are no more than three.) A pseudonym, when first used, may be followed by the author's real name, in brackets. For anonymous works of known or conjectured authorship, enclose the name in brackets. In the latter case, insert a question mark before the last bracket, e.g., [Daniel Defoe?]. See below, section 113.

Avoid repeating authors' names unnecessarily in footnotes. If "Max Fuchs" is cited in the text, the volume reference in the note should begin with the *title.* Avoid, if possible, the unnecessary repetition that results from splitting a name between the text ("Fuchs") and a footnote ("Max Fuchs"). In subsequent references, "Fuchs" alone is sufficient if no other author with the same surname is cited.

83 French names. French writers of both sexes often have several given names; but the form favored by the writer or by current usage should be used (e.g., Emile Faguet; Jean-Paul Sartre). For clarity, retain the hyphen used between given names (this is especially important in the case of compound surnames). Note that, whereas M.-J. Chénier stands for Marie-Joseph Chénier, M. R. Canat (a form often found on title pages) stands for *Monsieur* René Canat.

Check unfamiliar surnames on title pages of older books (through the early nineteenth century) for best spelling according to modern usage (l'Enclos—Lenclos; de Lille—Delille; Des Houlières—Deshoulières), and follow one form consistently. See also below, section 115.

Use the particle *de* after a given name (Guy de Maupassant) or a title (Mme de Staël; Abbé de Prades; the Marquis de Sade), but *not* with a surname alone (Musset; Tocqueville). Exceptions are surnames beginning with a vowel or mute *h* (D'Alembert; D'Holbach) and those pronounced as one syllable (De Gaulle; De Sèze; De Thou). American writers (unlike the French) commonly capitalize the particle in phrases such as "he asked De Gaulle," "a work by D'Urfé," while retaining the lower-case *de* after a given name or title (Charles de Gaulle; the Marquis d'Argenson). A particle that combines with an article is never omitted: one writes "the sonnets of Du Bellay," "a translation by Des Garets," "Maupassant's reference to the Chevalier Des Grieux." Occasional surnames are found to be indexed now one way and now another (Deffand—Du Deffand; Châtelet—Du Châtelet). The form that you prefer will determine whether you write, for example, "Mme du Deffand" or "Mme Du Deffand." Use one form consistently. See also below, section 115.

84 **Spanish names** are sometimes used in the full paternal-plus-maternal form (Ortega y Gasset), but more often a name will have contracted to the paternal form alone (Juan de Valdés) or to the paternal-maternal form without the conjunction (Blasco Ibáñez). Particles are treated as in French (Valdés is correct, not de Valdés). If, in a compound paternal name, the first name is "weak," i.e., commonplace and undistinguished (this includes most names in -*ez*, and the name García), the *last* name is often used in general reference, e.g., Pedro López de Ayala may be called Ayala (or by the full paternal name López de Ayala), but not López. Similarly, in a combined paternal-maternal name that has a "weak" paternal name, the maternal name may be used in general reference, e.g., Federico García Lorca may be referred to as Lorca (or by the full name García Lorca), but not as García.

Spanish names are discussed further in section 116.

85 **Names of institutions,** societies, agencies, etc., as given on a title page, may appear as author. See section 106, sample note 5, and section 120, paragraph 9.

86 **Title,** *in a work having no bibliography*, should, if of moderate length, be given the first time in full, e.g., Francois Froger,

A *Relation of a Voyage Made in the Years 1695-96-97 on the Coasts of Africa, Streights of Magellan, Brasil, Cayenna, and the Antilles*; Mary S. Locke, *Anti-Slavery in America, from the Introduction of African Slaves to the Prohibition of the Slave Trade (1619-1808)*. Include subtitle when practicable; but avoid cluttering your title with prolix matter found on some title pages. An extremely long title may be given in clear, short-title form, e.g., [Daniel Defoe], *The Life, Adventures, and Pyracies, of the Famous Captain Singleton . . .* (the remainder—over one hundred words—being omitted). In informal writing, or if mentioned incidentally, *Captain Singleton* would suffice.

If you have a bibliography, give title in sufficient detail to convey its contents, e.g., Francis Hall, *Travels in Canada, and the United States, in 1816 and 1817.* Part of a title such as *The Theatre, its Development in France and England, and a History of its Greek and Latin Origins,* may be omitted if it has no bearing on the subject you are treating. Most subtitles can be omitted. Many titles can be cited the first time in clearly abridged form (e.g., [Daniel Defoe], *Captain Singleton*; Emerson W. Gould, *Fifty Years on the Mississippi*) and expanded in the bibliography. The prime function of the latter would seem to minimize the need for ellipsis signs in footnote titles; but this is a matter of personal taste. Titles once cited may be simplified further in subsequent notes, e.g., Hall, *Travels.*

In a footnote relating to a title in the text, do not repeat that title verbatim or in abridged form; begin instead with the place of publication, a page reference, etc. (see section 106, sample note 1). Avoid so far as possible the expansion, in a footnote, of a short title cited in the text.

Title is followed by a comma unless the next detail is in parentheses.

If a chapter of a book or part of a volume by several authors is cited, it is enclosed in quotation marks (not underlined), followed by a comma and often by the word "in" preceding the volume title (see section 106, sample notes 11, 12). Chapter titles in books are rarely cited.

87 Editor's, compiler's, or translator's name is given in normal order, preceded by "ed.," "comp.," or "trans.," and followed by a comma unless the next detail is in parentheses. If particular reference is made, not to the text, but to an editor's or translator's technique, critical remarks, etc., this name may come first in the reference, followed by a comma and "ed." or "trans." In this case, title of the work comes next, followed by a comma, the word "by," and the author's name. (See section 106, sample notes 6, 8, 9, 11, 13-14 and remarks 15.)

88 Edition used, if not the first, is indicated in abbreviated form: 4th ed., rev. ed., new ed., etc. A comma follows unless the next detail is in parentheses. (See section 106, sample notes 4, 19.)

89 Series name or that of a particular edition may be omitted in a footnote if it occurs in the bibliography. Name is not underlined, and quotation marks or parentheses need not be used unless you are following a particular style. A comma follows unless the next detail is in parentheses. (See section 106, sample notes 9, 10.)

90 Number of volumes, usually omitted when reference is to specific volume(s) or if this detail is given in the bibliography, is written with Arabic number followed by "vols." and a comma, unless the next detail is in parentheses. (See section 106, sample note 2 and remark.)

91 Place of publication, publisher, date are written within parentheses followed by a comma.* These items, together with edition and page reference, may be omitted singly or in combination in references to well-known and frequently edited poems and plays (e.g., *The Deserted Village*; works by Shakespeare or O'Neill), also in standard reference works (encyclopedias, dictionaries, *DNB*, etc.). Facts of publication (place, publisher, date) may be omitted, in a paper or chapter, after the first citation, unless they serve a particular purpose.

92 Place of publication. For clarity and to avoid ambiguity, place name may be identified by country or state: compare

---

* For alternate forms when entire reference, including title, is in parentheses, see section 106, sample note 28 and remark.

> Cartagena, Colombia
> Bloomington, Ind.: Principia Press
> Bloomington: Indiana Univ. Press
> Cambridge, Mass., 1935
> Cambridge: Cambridge Univ. Press

It is often correct to list more than one place of publication (Boston & New York: Houghton Mifflin Co.) or to indicate joint publication (New York: The Modern Lang. Assoc. of America; London: Oxford Univ. Press). In some cases one place suffices (Chicago: Scott, Foresman & Co., omitting their offices at Atlanta, Dallas, and New York, though given on title page; New York: Holt, Rinehart & Winston, omitting Toronto and London if the book was printed in the United States).

Writers sometimes Anglicize foreign places of publication (Turin, Munich, The Hague, etc.), but in works dealing with European literature, or requiring more precise bibliographical description, original spellings are often preferred (Torino, München, La Haye, Genève, Londres, Francofurti, Oxonii, etc.).

Place of publication is followed by a colon if publisher's name is given, or by a comma if followed directly by the date. If place is not given on title page, supply it in brackets if it can be determined. If unknown, write "n.p."

93 Publishers' names are usually given in theses, also in any work that has no bibliography, and are often omitted in papers that provide these names in a list of references. They often furnish essential information, as in the case of a title printed in the same year or in the same city by two or more publishers. Sometimes they are given in titles of recent date and, in the same manuscript, omitted in those presumably out of print. (The dividing date is arbitrary: one may include publishers of works printed within, say, the last twenty years, or within the copyright period of fifty-six years.)

Names should be simplified: instead of "Librairie académique Perrin et Cie, libraires-éditeurs," write "Perrin et Cie," or simply "Perrin"; "Macmillan & Co." may be written "Macmillan." (Note use of ampersand and abbreviation "Co.")

Further abbreviation (e.g., New York Univ. Press) is common in some fields (including the humanities) but not in others.

94 Date is typed in Arabic numerals even if original is in Roman. If one or more volumes of a work have yet to appear, write the date thus: 1968 - -. If date is not given on title page, determine it, if at all possible, from other sources (copyright notice, library catalogues, etc.) and enter it in brackets. If conjectured, put a question mark before last bracket or write "[c. 1932]." etc. (See remark on "c." in section 104; also various specimens in sample footnote and bibliographical entries, and additional remarks in the next two sections.) If date is unknown, write "n.d.," without brackets.

95 Articles. The full title, in quotation marks, is followed by a comma, the name of the periodical (underlined, and often abbreviated), a comma, the volume number (in Roman capitals), the date (in parentheses), a comma, and the pagination, omitting "p." or "pp." Place of publication may be added in exceptional cases for clarification, e.g., *Hispania* (Madrid). For recent issues, the precise month or number may be included: (Nov., 1968), (Spring, 1968), in which the commas are optional; IV, No. 2 (1968) or IV, 2 (1968), though once a periodical is bound by volumes this detail usually serves no purpose. Dates *must* be so written if the periodical does not have consecutive pagination throughout the year (see section 106, sample notes 22, 23). If a periodical is published in more than one series, series number must be included, e.g., *The Library*, 5th ser., XV (March 1960), 10. The designation may also be Old Series or New Series (O.S., N.S. or, commonly, o.s., n.s.), sometimes placed before the volume number, sometimes after, e.g., *The American Monthly Magazine*, n.s., I (1836) or I, n.s. (1836).

For articles in newspapers and weeklies, give date, section number, page, and column, as needed, omitting volume number. (See section 106, sample notes 20, 25.)

96 Volume and page numbers. Write the former in Roman capitals, the latter in Arabic (except when small Roman is used for prefaces, etc.). The correct form for a work of more than one volume is III, 28-31, omitting "Vol." and "pp." (For exceptions, see title in next paragraph and section 106, sample notes 5, 7, 11.) In Greek and Latin works, comma may be omitted after both author and title. Note spacing and use of periods in the following: Cicero *De amicitia* XXVII.101; Plato *Republic* 546A; and, in biblical references, Judges XIX. 27-28 (or 19:27-28). Plays, works divided into cantos, etc., may be written similarly (e.g., *Macbeth* V.iii.22; *Inferno* X.87) or, more conventionally, *Macbeth*, V, iii, 22, etc.

The date of a particular volume of a work published over a period of years can, if desired, be shown thus: *The Letters of Sir Walter Scott*, VI (London, 1934), p. 8—*not* (London, 1934), VI, 8, for here the correct date would be 1932-37, that of the *edition*. A shorter form of this reference, when place is omitted, may be written thus: VI (1934), 8. (See section 106, sample notes 6, 7.)

In citing a single-volume work, and otherwise when no volume number is given, write "p. 11," "pp. 28-31," "Ibid., p. 5," etc. Note also: p. 28, n. 2; III, 28, n. 2. Page numbers cited from the same volume are separated by commas (e.g., pp. 2, 14, 34), references from different volumes by semicolons (e.g., I, 3, 5; II, 45).

An alternate system of notation is used in the *Readers' Guide to Periodical Literature* and in certain types of publication: *American Journal of Sociology*, 58:359-360, 1953. This and other variations may be acceptable in your field.

X

ABBREVIATIONS AND LATINISMS IN FOOTNOTES

97 Underlining. Note that the Latinisms below are not underlined for italics: this accords with the trend encouraged by the *MLA Style Sheet.*

98 Ibid. (for *ibidem,* "in the same place") is used to repeat *as much as possible* of a reference in the note immediately preceding:

⁵ Smith, *Works,* IV, 55.

⁶ Ibid., II, 21 (*not* "Smith, ibid., II, 21").

⁷ Ibid., p. 30 (*not* "Ibid., II, 30").

⁸ Ibid.

Do not use "ibid." if the note preceding contains more than one title.

99 Op. cit. (for *opere citato,* "in the work cited"), referring to one of several titles cited in a note immediately preceding or (usually) to a title in an earlier note, has fallen into some disfavor, for its overuse easily results in ineffectual pedantry. If an author's name appears in the text, a footnote reference "Op. cit., p. 5" is correct, although the simpler form "p. 5" suffices and is even preferable in annotating a compact series of quotations from the same work. If the author's name is not given or plainly inferred from the text, the form "Pope, p. 5" is recommended (here an added "op. cit." is clearly redundant).

Do not force the reader, by a careless use of "op. cit." or notes like "Pope, p. 5," to search back more than a page or two for the title in question; instead, repeat the title or use a short title (see section 106, sample notes 3, 7, 8). *Check this point carefully in your manuscript.* Do not use "op. cit." to refer to a title cited in a previous chapter, or to repeat the title of a periodical when reference is to another author.

100 Loc. cit. (for *loco citato*, "in the place cited") may be used with or without the author's name to repeat an entire reference. It should not substitute for "ibid.," should not be followed by a page reference (here the author's name or "op. cit." would be used), and should not refer to a previous "loc. cit." unless the full citation appears on the same or preceding page. *Example*:

16 Paul Nettl, "Goethe and Mozart," in *Goethe Bicentennial Studies*, p. 83.
17 Thomas, p. 3.
18 Nettl, loc. cit.

A specific title must be added in note 18 if more than one work by Nettl has thus far been cited.

101 Idem ("the same") is a conventional device for repeating an author's name. In notes at the foot of the page, it should refer only to matter on the same or preceding page. Its use by American writers has decreased markedly in favor of repeating the name itself.

102 Passim and cf. Use "passim" sparingly: specific page references are preferable. Avoid the use of "cf." (for *confer*, "compare") when "see" is intended.

103 Abbreviating titles, etc. Titles, editions, manuscripts, libraries, and even authors cited many times may be abbreviated or otherwise simplified by symbols, key letters, etc., provided that your preface or any early footnote explains the method followed. (See section 106, sample notes 17, 18.) Titles of familiar periodicals and reference works are commonly abbreviated (e.g., *HR, Hispanic Review; TLS*, [London] *Times Literary Supplement; DNB, Dictionary of National Biography*); see list preceding the annual bibliographical number of *PMLA* or periodicals in your field. In a paper that has no bibliography, or in any work that contains titles that the reader will possibly not comprehend in abbreviated form, it is well to write full titles the first time cited. Often it suffices to use abbreviations in the footnotes, and full titles in the bibliography. If the number of journals is large, or if abbreviations have to be devised, insert an explanatory list after the preface, or even at the beginning of the bibliography if abbreviations are used there also.

104 Some common abbreviations. Note the form, spacing, punctuation, and capitalization of the following:

abr. (abridged; abridgment)

Act IV, sc. iv (or Sc. II in a play not divided into acts)

A.M. or a.m.

anon. (anonymous)

art., arts. (article, articles)

b. (born)

biog. (biography, biographer, biographical)

Bk. VI, Bks. VI, IX

c. or ca. (*circa*, with dates; do not use in sense of "copyrighted"); "c. 1550" implies a closer approximation than does "1550?"

Chap. VI (or, occasionally, vi), Chaps. VI-VII (or, occasionally, chap., chaps.; ch., chs.)

col., cols. (column, columns)

comp. (compiler; compiled by)

d. (died)

diss. (dissertation)

ed., eds. (edition, editions; editor, editors; edited by)

ed. cit. (edition cited)

esp. (especially, as in "see esp. Chap. II")

f.,ff.: fac. or facsim. (facsimile)

fasc. (fascicle)

fig., figs. (figure, figures)

fl. (*floruit*, he or she flourished)

fol., fols. or foll. (folio, folios)

illus. (illustration; illustrated)

l., ll. (line, lines, preferably spelled out to avoid confusion with numerals)

MS, MSS (MS takes a period when referring to a specific manuscript, e.g., MS. E)

n., nn. (note, notes)

n.d. (no date)

n.p. (no place)

n.s., or, less often, N.S. (new series; capitalize for New Style)

No., Nos., no., nos.

o.s., or, less often, O.S. (old series; capitalize for Old Style)

pp. 25 f. (or better, pp. 25-26; pp. 25, 26); pp. 25 ff. (i.e., p. 25 and several pages following; inferior sometimes to notation of exact pages)

par., pars. (paragraph, paragraphs)

pl., pls. (plate, plates)

Pt., Pts., pt., pts. (part, parts)

pub. or publ., pubs. (published; publication, publications)

rev. (revised, revised by; review, reviewed by)

s.v. (*sub verbo* or *voce*, "under the word——")

Sec., Secs., sec., secs. (section, sections)

ser., or, less often, Ser. (series)

sig., sigs. (signature, signatures)

sig. C5^r or 5r (recto), 5^v or 5v (verso)

st., sts. (stanza, stanzas)

trans. or tr. (translator; translated by)

Vol. X, Vols. X-XI

vs. or v. (versus)

vss., vss., or v., vv. (verse, verses)

American writers often prefer the following forms to the alternatives given in parentheses:

above (supra; ante)

and others (et al.)

below (infra; post)

ff. (et seq.)

n.d. (s.d., for *sine die*)

n.p. (s.l., for *sine loco*)

see (vide)

to wit (sc. or scil., for *scilicet*)

105 Beginning of note. At the beginning of a footnote or sentence, some writers prefer "Page," "Pages," "Line," "Lines," etc., to "P.," "Pp.," "L.," "Ll.," etc., as being more pleasing to the eye.

XI

SAMPLE FOOTNOTE REFERENCES

106 Sample footnotes. The following footnotes illustrate various points covered above.

[1]Norman L. Torrey, The Spirit of Voltaire (New York: Columbia Univ. Press, 1938), p. 58. [If both author's name and title appeared in the text, the note would begin with the first parenthesis: (New York, etc.)]

[2]John Morley, Diderot and the Encyclopaedists, 2 vols. (London: Macmillan, 1897). ["New York" might be added; but this edition was printed in England. In a commoner type of note, followed by a page reference, "2 vols." would normally be omitted; but if needed, the note would then read: . . . Encyclopaedists (2 vols.; London: Macmillan, 1897), I, 10]

[3]Diderot, II, 73-75. [Short-title form of citation in n. 2]

[4][Noël-Antoine Pluche], Histoire du ciel . . . , 2nd ed. (Paris, 1740), I, 80. [Anonymous work. Abridged title might be expanded if not given later in bibliography]

[5]Smithsonian Institution, Smithsonian Treasury of Science, ed. Webster P. True (New York: Simon & Schuster, [1960]), I, 40.

[6]Shelley, Complete Works, ed. R. Ingpen & W. E. Peck (New York, 1926-30), IV (1928), 73. [Rather full form, suggesting first reference in notes. Volume date usually omitted]

[7]Shelley, Works, IV (New York, 1928), p. 73. [Simplified form, again specifying date of a particular volume. Note use of "p."]

[8]Works, ed. Ingpen & Peck, IV, 73. [The same, further simplified]

[9]Jean de La Bruyère, OEuvres, ed. Servois, Les Grands Ecrivains français (Paris, 1912), I, 3. [Work in a series]

[10]John Robert Moore, Defoe's Sources for "Robert Drury's Journal," Indiana Univ. Publications, Humanities Series No. 9 (Bloomington: Indiana Univ., 1943), pp. 22-23. [Title within title; work in a series]

[11]William F. Bottiglia, "Voltaire's Candide: Analysis of a Classic," in Studies on Voltaire and the Eighteenth Century, ed. Theodore Besterman, Vol. VII (Genève: Institut et Musée Voltaire, 1959), p. 8. [This, and n. 12, represent individual contributions in a series or volume by various authors]

[12]Frank E. Farley, "The Dying Indian," in Kittredge Anniversary Papers (Boston, 1913), pp. 251-53. ["In" may be omitted here, also in n. 11]

[13]Joseph Addison, Works, ed. Tickell (London, 1721), I, xii. [Usual reference to an author's edited works. Cf. the next note]

[14]Thomas Tickell, ed., Works, by Joseph Addison (London, 1721) . . . . [Here the reference concerns the editor's contribution rather than Addison's writings. If both figure in several references, use the form shown in n. 13]

[15]Otis E. Fellows and Norman L. Torrey, eds., The Age of Enlightenment: An Anthology of Eighteenth-Century French Literature (New York: Crofts, 1942), p. 21. [Or, F. S. Crofts & Co. Colon and hyphen added in title. Cited in later notes as Age of Enlightenment]

[16]Margaret L. Pflueger, "The Influence of Montaigne on Rousseau's First Discourse" (diss., Ohio State Univ., 1941), p. 3. [Quotation marks with unpublished material]

[17]Bibliothèque Inguimbertine de Carpentras (hereafter called Carp.), MS. 1871, fol. 81.

[18]Carp. 1871, fol. 111. [Simplified form of n. 17]

[19]Encyclopaedia Britannica, 13th ed., art. "Paper."
[Standard works require minimal publication data. An alternate, more explicit form: "Paper," Encyclopaedia Britannica,
13th ed., XIX, 725 (or, Vol. XIX, omitting page number). If
author's name is important, such a reference may begin: Thomas
Babington Macaulay, "Goldsmith, Oliver," etc. References to
editions after the 14th (1929), which are unnumbered, may be
written thus: (Chicago, 1961), V, 25]

[20]Chicago Tribune, Nov. 10, 1943, p. 24, col. 4. [Standard
newspaper reference. See also n. 25]

[21]E. E. Stoll, "Symbolism in Coleridge," PMLA, LXIII
(1948), 263. [Standard periodical reference]

[22]William R. Parker, "Report of the Delegate to the American Council of Learned Societies," PMLA, LXXIII (April 1958),
30. [Unlike the regular issues, this April (bibliographical)
number has separate pagination, therefore the month is added.
Cf. the next two notes]

[23]Atlantic Monthly, CCXI (June 1963), 64.

[24]Deutsche Zeitung, V (Oct. 4, 1950), 5.

[25]Time, Mar. 17, 1947, p. 59. [The commoner weeklies,
like newspapers, are usually cited without volume number, and
parentheses are omitted around dates]

[26]Desfontaines, Le Nouveau Gulliver (1730), as quoted in
Leonora C. Rosenfield, From Beast-Machine to Man-Machine (New
York: Oxford Univ. Press, 1941), p. 183.

[27]R. M. Smith, "Three Interpretations of Romeo and Juliet,"
South Atlantic Bulletin, XXIII (1948), 60-77, after summar-
izing three "conflicting interpretations" which prevail among
critics, rejects them one by one and concludes: "Do we . . . ?"
[Illustrates source placed at beginning of note. See n. 28 for
interpolated reference enclosed in parentheses; also nn. 29, 30]

[28]C. D. Locock (Poems of Shelley, London, 1911, II, 280,
529), following Mrs. Shelley's second collected edition (1839),
prints them as two. [Also correct, though more troublesome:
C. D. Locock (Poems of Shelley [London, 1911], II, 280, 529),
etc. Similarly, a periodical reference in parentheses may be
written: (. . . FR, XXXVI, 1963, 459)]

[29]He states (p. 10) that he had "heard rational men . . . ."

[30]In III, 9, he says: "London was . . . ."

[31]"Soon after his return in 1842, he was tried by a Court Martial . . ." (DNB).

[32]And perhaps editor-in-chief, if that is what Boswell's "engaged . . . to superintend" means (Hill-Powell, I, 307). [Or, . . . means. Hill-Powell, I, 307. Follow one style consistently. Although references in nn. 31 and 32 are put at the end (the less awkward position), the form shown in nn. 27-30 is generally preferred if practicable]

[33]". . . a high degree of taste . . ." (ibid., p. 5).

[34]". . . a high degree of taste . . . ." (Ibid., p. 5.) [In the last two examples, note the change in ellipsis sign, capitalization, and closing period. Follow one style consistently]

XII

BIBLIOGRAPHY

107 Placement. In published works, bibliographies in some fields are distributed by chapters, and in critical editions they often follow the introduction. In theses, they are traditionally put at the end.

108 Heading. Since relatively few studies offer in the bibliography section an exhaustive list of works by a given author, or on a given subject, the heading "Bibliography" may be both overpretentious and inaccurate. Choose therefore a more precise heading such as "Works Cited," "List of References, Partially Annotated," "Selected List of References," "Selected Bibliography," "Sources Consulted," etc.

Type heading, in capitals, on the twelfth line from top of page. Begin first entry five spaces below heading, or below a possible statement explaining abbreviations, omissions, and other special features. (Such remarks, set three spaces below heading, are single-spaced and run from left to right margin.)

109 Contents. The bibliography must contain every work cited (i.e., quoted or adduced as evidence or authority) in the text and footnotes, with the exception of primary sources quoted from secondary sources, and sources of incidental allusions, familiar quotations, etc., inclusion of which would be mere pedantry. It may also contain (except under the heading "Works Cited") works consulted but not used or quoted.

For easy reference, all entries—primary and secondary printed sources, journals, occasional manuscripts—can usually be put in a single section; but a separation of disparate material (printed and manuscript sources, public documents, news articles, editorials, reports, decrees, etc.) is sometimes desirable, especially if the number of items is large. For best form, consult works in your field. Another common division consists of works about an author, and works by the author. Division headings (if any) are centered on page, the important words capitalized, with triple spacing before and after. They need not be numbered or underlined.

110 Annotation. Brief annotations enhance the value of many bibliographies. See section 120, entries Sainte-Beuve in paragraph 3 and Weintraub in paragraph 7, also the several volumes of Cabeen (ed.), *A Critical Bibliography of French Literature* (Syracuse University Press), the source of these examples.

111 Form. Begin each entry at left margin, indent subsequent lines of the same entry from three to five spaces, and single space. Double space between entries. Do not carry over part of an entry to the next page. First page may be numbered at bottom margin.

112 Author's name is written with the surname first, and is followed by a period. Use the name by which the author is best known (for particulars, refer to section 82), and replace a first initial, if possible, by a given name (e.g., Smith, A[bner] B.) as an aid to the reader in using library card catalogues.

Use cross references for (*a*) hyphenated surnames (e.g., Jones, Edward Burne-. *See* Burne-Jones, Edward); (*b*) writers known by two names (e.g., Seton-Thompson, Ernest. *See* Seton, Ernest Thompson; Beaconsfield, Benjamin Disraeli, 1st Earl of. *See* Disraeli, Benjamin) or who have written under two names (e.g., Canfield, Dorothy. *See* Fisher, Dorothy Canfield; Saineanu, Lazar. *See* Sainéan, Lazare); (*c*) persons who, having legally changed their names, continue to publish; (*d*) prominent authors whose real names and pen names are equally well known (see section 113); (*e*) names that the reader might not find immediately by reason of subtleties in spelling or form (e.g., Decker, Thomas. *See* Dekker, Thomas; Morgan, Augustus de. *See* De Morgan, Augustus).

113 Anonymous authors; pseudonyms. In anonymous works, any intimation of authorship on title page should be included (see section 120, paragraph 10, sample entries *Literary Amusements* and *Le Mari silphe*). If a work is signed only with initials, enter these in lieu of full name, e.g., enter A.B.S. as S., A.B., or, if name is known, S[mith], A[bner] B. If a name is represented by asterisks or some other typographical device, enter the title only, followed by "By the Marquis of * * *," etc. Enter anonymous works of known or presumed authorship as follows: [Defoe, Daniel], or [Defoe, Daniel?].

There is no clear-cut principle governing entries of pseudonymous works; the *Encyclopaedia Britannica*, for example, contains articles on Owen Meredith and Novalis, whose real names (Lytton and Hardenberg) are main entries in the Library of Congress catalogue. Use as your main entry the name to which your reader will presumably turn first, e.g., a familiar assumed name such as Anatole France, Gorki, Meredith, Novalis, or Voltaire. The more obvious pen names are often referred to the real name (e.g., Mark Twain to Clemens, Boz to Dickens). Cross references from the author's real name are sometimes useful (e.g., Clemens—Twain), sometimes not (e.g., Thibault—Anatole France; Arouet—Voltaire). The correct form of entry is Graham, Tom [Sinclair Lewis]; or, Graham, Tom, pseud. of Sinclair Lewis. If, in this example, other titles are listed under Lewis, a pseudonymous title may be included with these, adding brackets ([Lewis, Sinclair] or, when name is repeated, [————]) and, following the title, "By Tom Graham." The pseudonym entry would then read Graham, Tom. *See* Lewis, Sinclair.

114 Repeated name. To repeat an author's name, type a solid line from five to seven spaces long, starting at left margin and ending with a period. Arrange titles by a single author alphabetically (including collected works, contrary to usual library cataloguing system) unless there is good reason for choosing a chronological order. Both styles should not be used in the same section. If there are one or more titles by Arnold B. Smith, and another by the same Smith in collaboration with Tracy R. Jones, enter this title last as follows: ————, and Tracy R. Jones. (Or, Jones, Tracy R.; see section

120, paragraph 5, third entry and remark.) This would be followed by works by Smith and *two* collaborators, etc. In listing like names, the simpler forms precede the more complex: Jones, John, precedes Jones, John Thomas.

115 French names that include the particle *de* are alphabetized thus: Aubigné, Théodore-Agrippa d'; Gaulle, Charles de; La Place, Pierre-Antoine de; Maupassant, Guy de. Names in which *de* is combined with the article (Des Barreaux; Du Guesclin), and Anglicized forms (De la Mare; De Selincourt), are alphabetized under *D*.

Down to the early nineteenth century, authors' names on title pages are often at variance with modern usage, and unreliable as guides to correct listing. Typical cases are (*a*) names that now include a once separate particle (Abbé de Lille—Delille; Des Essarts—Desessarts); (*b*) those that now include a once separate definite article (Le Sage—Lesage; Le Tourneur—Letourneur), with numerous exceptions such as Mme de La Fayette; La Fontaine; La Salle; (*c*) compound surnames, usually alphabetized under the first name (Dupont de Nemours; Fabre d'Eglantine; Martin du Gard; Petit de Julleville), but sometimes under the last name (Arnaud, Baculard d'; Bachaumont, Petit de; Saint-Gelais, Mellin de), and often, depending upon which biographical dictionary, bibliography, or library catalogue one consults, both ways, as in the case of Bernardin de Saint-Pierre—Saint-Pierre, Bernardin de; (*d*) titled persons, generally listed thus: Aubignac, François Hédelin, Abbé d'; Hauteroche, Noël Le Breton, Sieur de; but there are exceptions such as Duvergier de Hauranne, Jean, Abbé de Saint-Cyran; Vauquelin de La Fresnaye, Jean, Sieur des Yveteaux.

Note also the following entry forms: Aimé-Martin, Louis-Aimé, *called* (or *known as*); or, Aimé-Martin, Louis. *See* Martin, Louis-Aimé; Delisle de Sales, Jean-Claude Isoard, *called*; Gaussin, Jeanne-Catherine Gaussem, *called*.

For further guidance, one would do well to start with the Larousse encyclopedias and the catalogue of the Bibliothèque Nationale. Occasional disagreements, especially in categories (*c*) and (*d*), above, are handled by means of cross references, e.g., Choderlos de Laclos, Pierre. *See* Laclos, Pierre Choderlos de; Saint-Cyran, Abbé de. *See* Duvergier de Hauranne, Jean.*

116 Spanish names in their full form consist of given name (José) plus paternal name (Ortega) plus conjunction (y) plus maternal name (Gasset). While this form is usual in some instances, most names drop the conjunction and the maternal name (e.g., Lázaro Cárdenas; Juan de Valdés; Pedro Calderón de la Barca). Another common simplification consists in dropping only the conjunction, thus bringing together the paternal and maternal names (e.g., Vicente Blasco Ibáñez; Manuel Avila Camacho). As a general rule, alphabetize Spanish names by the paternal name only, treating particles in the same way as the French particle *de*. The foregoing names would be listed as follows:

> Avila Camacho, Manuel
> Blasco Ibáñez, Vicente
> Calderón de la Barca, Pedro
> Cárdenas, Lázaro
> Ortega y Gasset, José
> Valdés, Juan de

Names like José Léon Toral, Estéban Manuel de Villegas, and Carlos Antonio López cannot be alphabetized correctly until one determines whether the second name is the paternal name, or a second given name. In a combined paternal-maternal name like Federico García Lorca, having a "weak" paternal name (explained above, section 84), the maternal name (Lorca) is used so commonly for general reference that in bibliography and indexing it is well to use cross references: Lorca, Federico García. *See* García Lorca, Federico.

For further guidance consult the Espasa-Calpe *Enciclopedia universal ilustrada europeo-americana* and Library of Congress cards.

117 German, Dutch, and Flemish names that include the particles *von, am, zur, van, ten*, etc., are alphabetized thus: Arnim, Bettina von; Böhm von Bawerk, Eugen; Bülow, Dietrich

* See also my article "French Proper Names: A Guide to Correct Usage," *The Modern Language Journal*, L1 (1967), 344-46.

Heinrich, Freiherr von; Graff, Regnier de; Harr, Bernard ter; Hoff, Jacobus van den. Names of persons living and writing in the United States and in Great Britain usually begin with the particle: von Engeln, Oskar Dietrich; Von Holst, Hermann Eduard; Van Doren, Carl; van Loon, Hendrik Willem. In the latter group, verify personal preferences as regards capitalization of the particle, and use cross references for all except well-known writers, e.g., Eyck, Andrew ten. *See* Ten Eyck, Andrew.

In the United States and England, encyclopedias, dictionaries, biographical compilations, bibliographies, and scholarly books usually depart from the rule that German names written with an umlaut (*ä, ö, ü*) should be listed as though spelled out (*ae, oe, ue*); but in library catalogues the entry Müller (Mueller) will generally precede Muir, etc.

For further guidance consult foreign biographical dictionaries and encyclopedias (e.g., *Der grosse Brockhaus*) and Library of Congress cards.

118 Details. The amount of bibliographical detail required in an entry will be determined by the nature of the study. It is usually unnecessary to enter excessively long titles, the format (fol., 8vo, etc.), authors of prefaces and introductions, or the pagination of books. Articles, however, show complete pagination as well as continuations in later numbers or volumes (see section 120, entry Henderson in paragraph 12). In a bibliography containing many titles published in one place, the name may be omitted if so explained at the outset, e.g., "Place of publication is Paris unless otherwise noted." Except in special cases, record the total number of volumes in a multivolume work rather than particular volumes cited in footnotes. (Cf., in section 120, paragraph 3, entries Channing and Sainte-Beuve; paragraph 4, entries Mirabeau and Voltaire.)

In a bibliography entry, retain the same order of details as prescribed above for footnote references; but list the author's last name first, and use periods rather than commas to separate the main parts of the entry, i.e., author, title (book or article), and facts of publication. Omit parentheses with the latter. Treat missing data, conjectures, etc., as in footnotes.

Enter anonymous works under their titles, not under a section labeled "Anonymous." Retain initial articles in titles, but alphabetize under the next word, e.g., list *A Voyage* . . . under V. In foreign works, English "ed.," "trans.," "vols.," "introduction by," etc., may be used instead of their foreign equivalents. Foreign places of publication are discussed above, section 92. For further technical discussion, see Ronald B. McKerrow, *An Introduction to Bibliography for Literary Students* (Oxford: Clarendon Press, 1928), and Fredson Bowers, *Principles of Bibliographical Description* (New York: Russell and Russell, 1962).

119 Checking. As a final and most important step, compare each title cited in your footnotes with the corresponding entry in the bibliography. Failure to do so will invariably result in omissions, discrepancies, and errors in various details.

XIII

SAMPLE BIBLIOGRAPHY ENTRIES

120 Sample bibliography entries. The following examples illustrate common types of bibliographical entry and their styling.

1. Edited or translated works:

> Dante Alighieri. The Divine Comedy of Dante Alighieri, trans. J. A. Carlyle, Thomas Okey, and P. H. Wicksteed; Introd. by C. H. Grandgent. The Modern Library. New York: Random House, 1932. [Less formally, "Dante," since "Alighieri" recurs in title. Grandgent's introduction is included because of this scholar's eminence in Dante studies]

> Dictionary of Political Economy, ed. R. Palgrave. 3 vols. New York: Macmillan, 1901-8. [Or, Sir Robert Palgrave, although the simpler form serves its purpose here]

> Fordham, Elias P. Personal Narrative of Travels . . . 1817-1818, ed. F. A. Ogg. Cleveland: A. H. Clark Co., 1906. [Length of title warrants abridgment here]

> Leslie, Charles. Histoire de la Jamaïque, trans. Raulin. 2 vols. Londres, 1751.

> Teuffel, Wilhelm Sigmund. History of Roman Literature, rev. & enlarg. Ludwig Schwabe; trans. George C. W. Warr. 2 vols. London: George Bell & Sons, 1900.

2. Works in a series:

> The Aufère Papers: Calendar and Selections, ed. Winifred Turner. Publications of the Huguenot Society of London, No. 40. London: Frome, Butler & Tanner, 1940.

Bowers, David F., ed. Foreign Influences in American
    Life: Essays and Critical Bibliographies. Princeton
    Studies in American Civilization, Vol. II. Princeton:
    Princeton Univ. Press, 1944.

Judson, Alexander C. Sidney's Appearance: A Study in
    Elizabethan Portraiture. Indiana Univ. Publications,
    Humanities Series No. 41. Bloomington: Indiana Univ.
    Press, 1958.

König, Karl. Ueberseeische Wörter im Französischen
    (16.-18. Jahrhundert). Beihefte zur Zeitschrift für
    romanische Philologie, No. 91. Halle: Max Niemeyer
    Verlag, 1939. [Or, omit "Verlag"]

3. Part (chapter, essay, etc.) of a work or series:

Channing, Edward. The Jeffersonian System, 1801-1811, Vol.
    XXI of The American Nation: A History, ed. A. B. Hart.
    New York: Harper & Bros., 1906. [Essentially a
    separate book, though in a multivolume work, this title
    is italicized; cf. the next two entries]

Feise, Ernst. "Zum Problem von Goethes Clavigo," Studies
    in German Literature in Honor of Alexander Rudolph Hohl-
    feld. Univ. of Wisconsin Studies in Language and Lit-
    erature, No. 22. Madison, 1925. ["In" may be used
    before "Studies." Page numbers are not essential,
    though some writers prefer to include them]

Sainte-Beuve, Charles-Augustin. "Les Confessions de
    J.-J. Rousseau," in his Causeries du lundi, III, 78-97.
    Paris: Garnier, n.d.
    Excellent analysis of originality of style of Confessions:
    naturalness, realism, occasional archaisms, and charm.
    (Dated Nov. 4, 1850.) [Essay in a collection; annotated
    entry (see also Weintraub in paragraph 7)]

4. Foreign titles:

Eslava y Elizondo, H. Breve memoria histórica de la mú-
    sica religiosa en España. Madrid, 1860.

Göpfert, Herbert Georg. "Der Dichter und das Drama unserer
    Zeit." Neue Literatur, XXXVIII (1937), 231-34.

_____. Paul Ernst und die Tragödie. Diss., Greifswald.
    Leipzig, 1932. [Published; cf. Wycoco in paragraph 11]

Massini Ezcurra, José M. El cancionero argentino. Santa
Fe, Arg., 1956. [Identification of place name added]

Mirabeau, Victor Riquetti, Marquis de. L'Ami des hommes,
ou Traité de la population. New ed., 5 vols. Avignon,
1762.

Restori, A. "Per la storia musicale dei trovatori proven-
zale." Rivista musicale italiana, III (1896), 407-51.

Voltaire, François-Marie Arouet de. OEuvres complètes,
ed. Moland. 52 vols. Paris: Garnier, 1877-85.

[See also Metchenko in paragraph 12]

5. Several works by one author:

Fellows, Otis E. French Opinion of Molière (1800-1850).
Brown Univ. Studies, Vol. III. Providence: Brown
Univ., 1937.

_____. Review of Diderot, The Testing Years, 1713-1759,
by Arthur M. Wilson. FR, XXXI (1958), 579-81.

_____, and Norman L. Torrey, eds. The Age of Enlighten-
ment: An Anthology of Eighteenth-Century French Literature. New York: F. S. Crofts & Co., 1942. [Colon and
hyphen added. Note that second name follows footnote
style. Some authors and manuals (e.g., Chicago)
prefer to give surname first]

Gwilliam, John. The Exile of Elba: A Poem . . . . London,
[1814].

_____. The Imperial Captive; or, The Unexampled Career
of the Ex-Emperor, Napoleon . . . . 2 vols. London,
1817.

6. Works by two or more authors: see the third entry in preceding paragraph, and Metchenko in paragraph 12.

7. Data supplied in brackets:

Benezet, Anthony. Short Observations on Slavery, Introductory to some Extracts from the Writings of the Abbé
Raynal . . . . N.p., [1770?]. [Or, "c. 1770," in
brackets]

[Fisher, Charles Edward?]. Kanzas [sic] and the Constitution. Boston: Damrell & Moore, 1856.

Schiller, Friedrich. Werke . . . , ed. E. Jenny. 10 vols. [Basel: Birkhäuser, 1945.] [Redundancies in titles (here, Schillers Werke) are usually avoided]

W[eintraub], S[tanley], ed. "St. Pancras Manifesto." Shaw Review, III, No. 1 (1960), 21-31. Text of a political tract by G. B. Shaw and Sir William Geary. [Annotated entry. Also correct: III, 1 (1960), etc.]

[See also British Museum in paragraph 9]

8. Descriptive, rather than actual, title:

Bowe, Forrest L. [Bibliographical notes on early American translations from the French]. Papers of the Bibliographical Society of America, XXXV (1941), 70, 72, 159-61, 205-6.

[See also the second entry in paragraph 5]

9. Institution, organization, government, etc., as author:

British Museum, Department of Printed Books. Subject Index of the Modern Works Added to the Library of the British Museum [1881-1935]. . . , ed. G. K. Fortescue and others. 11 vols. London, 1902-37.

Great Britain, Parliamentary Papers. Report of the Committee of the House of Commons in Consequence of the Several Motions Relative to the Treatment of Prisoners of War . . . . London, 1798.

Philadelphia Bibliographical Center and Union Library Catalogue. Union List of Microfilms. Rev. ed. Supplement, 1949-52. Ann Arbor, Mich.: J. W. Edwards, 1953.

U.S. Congress. State Papers and Correspondence Bearing upon the Purchase of the Territory of Louisiana. 57th Congress, 2nd sess., House Document No. 431. Washington, 1903.

10. Anonymous works:

    "Daudet and Dickens." _LTLS_, May 11, 1940, p. 231. [Or, _The_
    (London) _Times Literary Supplement_]

    H., H.S. "The 'Lost' Sixth Douay Diary." _N&Q_, CLXXVI
    (1944), 84-86.

    Literary Amusements; Evening Entertainer. By a Female Hand.
    2 vols. Dublin: S. Price and others, 1782.

    Le Mari silphe, par M. F....C.A.L.P.d.T. Musique de M.
    Fournier. Toulouse: Jean Baour, 1775. [Probable in-
    terpretation: Monsieur F., collecteur à la porte de
    Toulouse]

11. Unpublished works:

    Musa, Mark. "Inferno, Canto XIX." Paper read before the
    Renaissance Club of Indiana University, Jan. 20, 1963.

    Wycoco, Remedios S. "The Types of North-American Indian
    Tales." Diss., Indiana Univ., May 1951.

12. Periodicals and annuals:

    Cowley, Malcolm. "Footnote on French Prosody." _New Re-
    public_, May 22, 1944, pp. 714, 716.

    Henderson, W. B. Drayton. "Montaigne's Apologie of Ray-
    mond Sebond and King Lear." _Shakespeare Assoc. Bull._,
    XIV (1939), 209-53; XV (1940), 40-54.

    Metchenko, A., A. Dement'ev, and G. Lomidze. "For a Pro-
    found Elaboration of the History of Soviet Literature"
    ("Za glubokuyu razrabotku istorii sovetskoj literatury").
    Kommunist, No. 13, 1956, pp. 83-100. [Translated and
    transliterated title. Use same form (without under-
    lining) in translating book titles]

    Muirhead, Arnold. "A Jeremy Bentham Collection." _The
    Library_, 5th ser., I (1947), 6-27.

    Steen, J. van der. "Vondels Jempsar en de Slang." _De
    Nieuwe Taalgids_, LIII (1959), 326-32.

Takahashi, Atsuko. "A Study of Theodore Dreiser's Thought." Essays and Studies in British and American Literature (Tokyo Woman's Christian College), VII (Summer 1959), 71-102. [Model for lesser-known publications: place of origin added]

Thompson, Wade Clayton. "The Aesthetic Theory of Henry David Thoreau." DA, XX (1960), 3756 (Columbia). [Dissertation abstract]

13. Encyclopedias; standard reference works:

"Goldsmith, Oliver." Encyclopaedia Britannica. 14th ed., X, 494-98. [Or, Vol. X (omitting page numbers)]

"Gosset, Isaac." DNB, VIII, 261-62.

Macaulay, Thomas Babington. "Goldsmith, Oliver." Encyclopaedia Britannica, [etc.].

THE CHANGING ATTITUDE TOWARD GEORG BÜCHNER

BY

ERWIN LOUIS MEYER

Submitted to the Faculty of the Graduate School
in partial fulfilment of the requirements
for the degree Doctor of Philosophy
in the Department of German
Indiana University
August, 1945

THE INFLUENCE OF RICHARD WAGNER

IN FRENCH LITERATURE

(1860 TO 1890)

BY

WARREN JERROLD WOLFE

Submitted to the Faculty of the Graduate School
in partial fulfilment of the requirements
for the degree Master of Arts in the
Department of French and Italian
Indiana University
May 1949

TABLE OF CONTENTS

Specimen Page 4

TABLE OF CONTENTS

CONTENTS

Page

Specimen Page 6

TABLE OF CONTENTS

Specimen Page 8

TABLE OF CONTENTS

CHAPTER X

THE SLAVERY QUESTION DURING THE REVOLUTIONARY
PERIOD, 1789-1794

During the last few years of the legal existence of
colonial slavery, humanitarian literature was significantly
expanded by several new works directed against the enslave-
ment of Negroes.[1] The views of the celebrated Thomas Clark-
son were presented anew in 1789 in the Idée de la traite et
du traitement des nègres and in an Essai sur les désavanta-
ges de la traite. The first thirty-one pages of the former
work contained extracts from his Latin dissertation on slavery,[2] and the remaining pages, on the treatment of slaves,
gave accounts and anecdotes of tortures and cruelties commonly witnessed in Santo Domingo.[3] The translator, Grama-
gnac, added twenty-five pages of introductory remarks. In
the same year the Abbé Nicolas Bergier published his Dictionnaire théologique, containing three articles ("Philosophes,"

---

[1] The familiar theme of the wretched South American Indians
was not, however, forgotten: see Drobecq's poem "Le Cacique et
le François," which appeared in the Almanach des Muses in 1789
(pp. 183-84); Poiret's Voyage en Barbarie (1789), I, 19.

[2] This competed in 1785 for the prize offered by Cambridge
University for an essay on the question Anne liceat invitos
in servitutem dare? An English translation, entitled An Essay on the Slavery and Commerce of the Human Species, was
published in London in 1786, and there were three French adap-
tations by 1789.

[3] The second extract "est l'essentiel d'un mémoire . . . en-
voyé à M. de Sartines, Ministre d'Etat, par un Préfet Aposto-
lique, alors dans la Colonie [Saint-Domingue]." This part
embraces 76 pages.

the authority of Simon Kenton, . . . says, 'Logan's form was striking and manly, his countenance calm and noble . . . .'"[24] More than seventy years later, Franklin B. Sawvel gives a similar, but embellished, description of Logan:

> Logan was now in the prime of life, a fine specimen of robust manhood with a commanding presence, dignified in bearing and brave as the bravest of the brave. He was built in the style of the primeval forest, six feet two or more, broad shouldered, lithe of limb and alert and as soft of tread as a tiger; he was self-reliant and straight as an arrow. He is described as handsome, with more than usual raven-trailing locks and as having jet-black eyes vigilant as the eyes of an eagle, firm-set mouth and the kindly features of a child.[25]

While these descriptions may have some basis in fact, they also suggest a confusion with a Captain James Logan, the warrior adopted by General Benjamin Logan--"a fine-looking fellow, six feet tall and splendidly formed, with courage of the highest quality" and capable of great "delicacy and kindness" to women and children.[26] In any event, it is easy to imagine that they are in some degree a romantic conception like that in "Lavinia's" poem:

> Brave was Logan, none were braver,
> Daring war by land and main;
> Tall was Logan, none were taller;
> Hail'd the Sachem of the plain.

---

[24] *The American Pioneer*, I (1842), 18.

[25] *Logan the Mingo*, p. 67. Sawvel was doubtless aware that Logan's Indian name (Tah-gah-jute) meant "his eyelashes stick out or above,"--"as if looking through or over something, and so well could mean 'spying'" (Hodge).

[26] Jacob P. Dunn, *True Indian Stories* . . . (Indianapolis, 1909), pp. 166, 168.

125

fable, Care (Cura) shaped a creature out of clay and Jupiter gave this shape a spirit or soul. Earth (Humus) was entitled to provide the name: a human being (Homo), according to Saturn's verdict. As to its rightful owner he decided: "After death Jupiter will receive the spirit, Earth the body. Care, however, since she first shaped this creature, shall possess it as long as it lives." ("Cura enim quia prima finxit, teneat quamdiu vixerit.")[86]

Burdach stresses the point that, according to this fable, man is "solange er lebt . . . das Kind der Sorge." But Faust has forfeited the nature of a free human being by concluding the pact with Mephistopheles. The "Uebermensch" Faust, he continues, "bleibt, seitdem er sich der Magie ergeben, frei von der Sorge."[87] "Aber," he goes on, "am Ende, nachdem er die düstere Macht der Magie innerlich überwunden, . . . steht er auf dem Weg 'ins Freie'. . . und deshalb . . . verfällt jetzt sein körperlicher Teil dem natürlichen Menschenlose, wird Eigentum der Erde."[88] By the latter Burdach means that

---

frequently that which spurs on, incites" (Harper). Stimulus even more than excitare means the spurring to some action. Gummere translates the above phrase with "routs us from our beds with the sharpest of goads" (Seneca, Ad Lucilium epistulae morales, with an English translation by Richard M. Gummere, Loeb Classical Library, New York, 1930, II, 427). The desperate deeds to which Sorge incites the rich and powerful are implied in Seneca's passage but not in Burdach's translation.

86. Burdach quotes only in German translation (pp. 41 f.). The Latin quotation is taken from Heidegger, p. 198.

87. Page 44.   88. Page 45.

121 Mailing the manuscript. "Book Manuscript" (or "Special 4th-Class") rate, insured, is safe, much cheaper than first-class, and, if marked "Special Handling," just as fast. Special Delivery service applies also. Express or parcel post (insured) are adequate, but slower. Pages should not be stapled together, folded, or bent. Paper clips may be used to separate sections. Photographs and other illustrations must be wrapped with special care as a safeguard against possible damage.

INDEX

Unless otherwise indicated, references are to numbered sections rather than to page numbers.